BEST OF
BASKETBALL
FROM
THE COACHING CLINIC

BEST OF
BASKETBALL
FROM
THE COACHING CLINIC

Compiled by the Editors of
The Coaching Clinic

PARKER PUBLISHING COMPANY, INC.
West Nyack, New York

Printed in the United States of America
07358—BC

INTRODUCTION

There's always one big problem when compiling "the best of anything"—and we faced it in compiling *Best of Basketball from THE COACHING CLINIC.*

The problem: When you pride yourself on publishing nothing but the best, month after month, how does one come up with a select group of basketball articles? One editor solved the problem immediately: "Reprint every basketball article and be done with it." Believe it or not, that's how we started.

Our initial manuscript was a meaty three volumes, at least—so we were forced to begin a process of elimination as a result of which we did the following:

• Made a note of every article that especially impressed us, our basketball consultant and coaches in the field.

• Restricted our selection to coaches, both high school and college, with impressive win-loss records.

• Checked the material for full-rounded coverage, choosing the most comprehensive articles on various phases of the game.

• Then arranged the material the way any good coach arranges his coaching plans—organizational duties, offensive and defensive strategy.

The final selection is here: 40 articles, clearly illustrated with over 200 line drawings, *Best of Basketball from THE COACHING CLINIC.* These top high school and college coaches bring you a storehouse of coaching ideas and techniques that have made them winners through the years—many of which can do the same for you.

The Board of Editors
THE COACHING CLINIC

v

CONTENTS

Part III

DEFENSIVE TECHNIQUES AND DRILLS

PART I

ORGANIZING A WINNING SEASON

1.

TIPS ON BUILDING A HIGH SCHOOL BASKETBALL PROGRAM

by BILL FOSTER

Head Basketball Coach
Rutgers University

Bill Foster moved into the head basketball coaching job at Rutgers University in 1964, with a 45–11 record behind him for his three years as coach at Bloomsburg (Pennsylvania) State College. Before Bloomsburg, he coached six years of (winning) high school ball.

Although a high school basketball coach cannot recruit, he can take definite affirmative steps to improve the quality of the players who turn out for his team. A well-planned feeder program, worked out with the help of other basketball coaches in the school system, is the way to do it. Here are some ideas on working out a good program.

• *The Basketball Syllabus:* To make a basketball program most effective, the teaching and thinking of each coach in the system must closely parallel those of the head coach in the high school. This is easy to say, but extremely difficult to achieve. I believe that the only way to get continuity of instruction is to prepare a basketball "syllabus" in booklet form that would be used throughout the

3

school system. The primary purpose of the booklet is to standardize the teaching of as many phases of basketball as is possible.

In many school systems it is difficult to get an experienced basketball coach to handle one of the lower grade level teams. The syllabus would also serve as an excellent guide, if properly prepared and utilized, to give an inexperienced coach tips and pointers on what to do and how to do it.

The syllabus should include what is to be taught, how it is to be taught, and the drills for mastering the skills. The teaching and the drills should be progressive in nature, beginning with the 5th grade coach demonstrating dribbling, shooting, passing, basic individual defensive stance, individual offensive moves, stopping and starting, and so on.

The preparation of the syllabus is only half of the job. The other, more important half, is to make sure that the booklet is properly utilized. This can be done by making sure that you get the full cooperation of all the other coaches in your system. If you let them all have a hand in making up the syllabus, you'll be surprised how willing they will be to go along with your ideas.

• *The Cumulative Folder:* This device is a permanent file that follows each player throughout his basketball career. It starts when he starts basketball and ends when he graduates from high school. In this folder, each coach places all possible information on the individual. This includes things such as the player's height and weight at the beginning and end of each school year, his IQ, basketball strong and weak points, each coach's remarks about him, and so on. Any other information pertaining to the boy is also placed in the cumulative folder.

The folder can either be called in by the high school's head coach in May of the school year, or it can be passed directly on to the player's next coach.

• *Statistics:* The development and adoption of a standardized set of statistical forms will make the organization of the entire program more effective. The form should include statistics such as field goals and foul shots made and taken, held balls, assists, defensive and offensive rebounds and lost balls on each of the players. Each coach throughout the system should send copies of the year's final statistics to the high school head coach and the boy's coach at the next level. The main use of the forms is to enable the coaches to make players more conscious of the importance of steals, loss of the ball, rebounds, turnovers, and areas other than scoring.

• *Staff Meetings:* All coaches are busy during the year, but at least two staff meetings each year should be arranged. This should be a time when the coaches at each level air their various problems. This way, the high school head coach will be constantly aware of the roadblocks at each level of the system. This is also a good time for the high school coach to offer to conduct, with the varsity players, a clinic for the benefit of the younger prospects and their coaches.

A list can be given to each of the coaches telling them of the various interest-building films put out by basketball manufacturers. These films are excellent motivational devices. They are easy to secure, and, for the most part, free of charge. A similar list telling each of the coaches of the new books out and the local coaching clinics that they can attend is a good idea.

• *Scrap Book:* An interesting gimmick designed to create more interest among the students (the younger ones especially) is the basketball scrap book. One scrap book can handle all the clippings on the basketball team from the beginning of the season to the end. A manager could handle the entire operation during the season. At the end of the season, the scrap book can be presented to the school library for permanent keeping.

The scrap book serves as a real interest-builder, and it gives the coach a permanent record.

• *Training Films:* The high school coach should not overlook the possibility of making a training film for use in the entire school system. This is especially workable in the larger systems. Pictures can be taken of the areas that should be standardized and the demonstrators should be the high school varsity squad members.

• *Playing Courts:* Not directly concerned with, but perhaps *the* biggest booster of any feeder program is the availability of playing locations. Virtually all high schools and junior high schools have a gym where indoor basketball facilities are available. Some school districts have provided outdoor courts at each of their school locations. If these have lights, they can serve as an excellent supplement to the indoor courts. If they don't, or if more courts are needed, the coach and the booster club must do the job.

A service organization might be glad to help out not only with finances, but manpower as well. Some schools have had their woodworking shops cut backboards out of plywood. These are then sold together with instructions on how to attach them to a garage, to interested parents—especially those who have elementary school boys.

2.

BUILDING A CHAMPIONSHIP COLLEGE BASKETBALL TEAM

by JACK GARDNER

Head Basketball Coach
University of Utah

At the University of Utah, Jack Gardner has the championship habit. For nine years he was the scourge of the now-defunct Skyline Conference: six titles, two seconds and a won-and-lost record of 102–24 (overall, 178–46). His teams are now a constant threat in the Western Athletic Conference. Jack Gardner is obviously a skilled coach; but as he says here, building a champion takes more than that. His over-all record to date is 528–216.

A coach's duties are not limited to the floor. To build winners, he must be an *organizer* and *administrator*. Forms, charts and checklists are a part of his life. These must detail his responsibilities, his coaching and game plans, schedule analysis, game management, trip information, player and staff meetings, equipment check, game charting, clinic outlines—all of these and more. He should break down, in writing, practice sessions, offenses, defenses, tactics, strategy, scouting and tournament play.

A project left untended goes to the dogs.

Here, in checklist form, are the things we do at Utah. I believe they have been invaluable in helping us achieve our record. I recommend them to all coaches. A lot of work? It sure is. Nobody ever won without work.

1. Basic Coaching Principles: You've got to be clear in your own mind *how* you are going to operate.

- We make our drills and practice *fun*. Driving players through monotonous drills is drudgery. We coach through friendly play-inspiring games.
- We give fundamentals top priority. Before we teach any style of play, we teach the skills: footwork, cutting, screening, passing, dribbling, shooting, guarding, rebounding.
- We permit discussion of fundamentals, offenses, and defenses— so long as it is not at the expense of diligent practice and development of team play.
- We teach driving, aggressive play—with the realization that it will lead to more mistakes and more fouling than in cautious play.

2. Drills: A drill which does not develop a game skill is of little value and may be harmful. We reverse the usual procedure: we start with a game offensive or defensive maneuver and then break it down so that it will constitute a drill. These break-down drills make up virtually all of our drill work.

3. Scrimmages: You can't develop team play without them. Since we find it difficult to scrimmage with "outside" teams, we run regular scrimmages between the varsity and frosh squads.

We get game experience by running scrimmages on a formal basis: regular officials, time-outs, between-halves procedures, *and* statisticians. It is a regular game.

4. Style of Play: I have studied, and continue to study, the different systems of leading coaches and evaluate them on the basis of my own experience. The result is that I have used practically the same offense and defense since the first day I started coaching.

To my basic system, of course, I have added various methods, plays and philosophies which blend in with my system and beliefs.

5. The Players: This is the big job. I feel that selecting superior players and welding them into a team is much more important than a style of play. I also feel strongly that a coach will be more successful if he picks the boy who "gives his all"—who puts out the entire game—than in picking the gifted boy who is intent on personal glory, and who may loaf in practice and games.

This latter type is usually important only in winning games you probably would have won without him. The player who fights all the way is the one who will win the tough games for you and put your team in the championship class.

6. Equipment: It goes without saying, I hope, that at Utah we try to select the best player equipment available: uniforms, warm-up suits, shoes, balls and other items. Comfort, attractiveness and durability are the important factors—in that order.

Don't underestimate attractiveness. You all know the warm, comfortable feeling you get when you wear a new, good-looking suit of clothes. This lift is no different from that a player gets in a colorful, well-fitting uniform.

7. Facilities: I know not all coaches are blessed with the best and most modern place to play. But you can do what we do at Utah: make sure that all facilities are well-lighted and spotless—dressing rooms, spectator seats, benches, and playing courts.

Yes, I repeat, this is part of building championship teams. This is part of your responsibility as a coach.

8. Rules: Obviously, all coaches must know the rules inside out. This is a must. We are very sure that the players know all of the rules that govern their play.

We devote an early practice session to the rules and the changes in the rules. During practices and scrimmages, we explain the application of the rules to the situations that develop.

9. Offense, Defense, Game Strategy: We prepare a complete outline of all offenses and defenses which we will use during the year. Before the first practice session, we check it over thoroughly.

Much of this comes out of pre-season meetings with my assistants. We go over, time and again, offenses, defenses, game tactics and strategies we expect to use. The outline is mimeographed for future use, and possible distribution to the players.

10. Practice Outlines: We prepare outlines for practice sessions. This helps assure that nothing is overlooked in preparing our teams. The outlines are in four groups: pre-season, in-season, post-season, and tournament.

In preparing our outlines, we use the records of the preceding season to help us determine the frequency and time allotments for the things we do in practice.

11. Clinics: I feel it is the duty of every coach to subscribe to the development of youngsters and to assist them in getting started *right*. They are the varsity players of the future. Since I do not feel it wise to add too much to the heavy program of the players, the duties fall on me and my assistants. We conduct a great number of clinics, and use the youngsters who attend as demonstrators.

12. Scouting: Before the season starts: (a) We get together all charts and records we have for each opponent and work out a complete scouting program. (b) We review all scouting forms and objectives and make any changes we feel will help us get better information.

13. Trips and Tournaments: Except for post-season tournaments based on a team's performance, we try to complete all trip and tournament information before the first practice session.

Utah plays a national schedule; this means that the players are forced to give up many student pleasures and vacations. We like to give them complete information on travel, hotel accommodations, and length of stay in various cities.

14. Charts and Statistics: "If it moves, we chart it." This is not a figure of speech at Utah; we mean it. We place great importance on our "look at the record" program. We study and analyze the preceding season's findings to see where we can improve. All charts and forms used to get information are discussed and new ones prepared.

Coaching a champion is a full-time job, every day of the year. When the coach leaves the practice floor, his job is just beginning.

3.

HIGH SCHOOL BASKETBALL SCOUTING

by Hardin McLane

Head Basketball Coach
Elizabethtown (Kentucky) Catholic High School

Hardin McLane's 6-year record as Head Basketball Coach at Elizabethtown Catholic High School is 140–31 which includes 3 district championships in a row. The school is small (male enrollment is less than 100), yet it has ranked among the top 15 in the state every year since Hardin McLane came there.

All basketball coaches realize the value of scouting their opponents. Too often, however, these coaches have not developed a well-organized scouting program *before* going to their games. If this is the case, the coach will accomplish very little. Here is how I organize my scouting program. It has proven to be an effective method for me, and I am sure it will for you.

• *Master Scouting Schedule:* Most high school coaches exchange copies of their schedules before the season begins. When you send each of the schools on your schedule a list of your games, you should ask the coaches to send you a copy of theirs. Once you get all these schedules, make a master scouting schedule. We make ours on a large sheet of cardboard where we rule off equal space for each month of the basketball season. When completed, it resembles a large five-month calendar, each day having its own block. We then write in all the games each opponent plays in the blocks on the nights we aren't playing—sometimes we have only one game to be scouted, other times we may have as many as seven or eight. Then, using another sheet of cardboard, we write all the dates and games to be scouted in order. This would result in something like this: Tuesday, December 6, City High at County High—7:30 P.M.; Friday, December 9, Smith High at Jones High—8 P.M.; and so on through March.

• *Scouting Forms:* One of the biggest aids to organization of the scouting effort is the pre-prepared scouting form. We write our report and never trust to memory since it may often be several weeks later when we meet the team being scouted. Going into the scouting report itself, we have definite things we look for each time we scout. When my assistant coach goes with me, he keeps shot charts, points scored, fouls, and offensive and defensive rebounds. Before going into the things I list on my own charts, I will explain the assistant's charts.

• *Assistant's Charts:* In the past, we kept a team shot chart, but in recent years we have broken this down in a better way. We now keep *individual shot charts* on each player in the top eight on the teams we scout. The assistant has eight smaller shot charts on one sheet of paper. At the top of each is a space for the player's name, number and position.

We use a number system to record shot types. For example, if a player shoots a lay-up, the number one is written on his chart at the spot on the floor from where the shot was taken. If the player hits the shot, the number is circled. Similarly, a right hand jump has a two, a left hand jump a three, and so on. All made shots are circled and at the end of the game, we have a record of each boy's shooting percentage, what shots he likes best and the spots on the floor from where he likes to shoot them.

The assistant also keeps *offensive and defensive rebounds* in order to help us determine what boys we have to block out on the boards. He keeps *fouls* to indicate the foul-prone players.

The chances of winning a particularly close game might result from getting one of their "stars" in foul trouble and having him spend most of his time on the bench. In addition, the assistant keeps *floor errors* or *"turn-overs"* to help us decide which boys can best stand pressure and which are prone to error—we prod the weak ones.

• **The Coach's Chart:** I keep two charts: one on the top eight players and another for general team comments. All of the following questions will be (I hope) answered on these charts. I look for answers to and insights into: individual player moves; patterns; defense; out-of-bounds plays; team strengths and weaknesses; player strength and weaknesses; jump ball and tip-off plays; size of players; speed aggressiveness; conditioning; bench strength; spirit; ball handling ability; shooting ability; do they switch or slide through on defense; do they play as a team or as individuals; how can we best beat them; do they press (full-court, ¾ court, half-court, man-to-man or zone); would a press hurt them; do they have weak links; do they hustle; should we fast break or control against them; are they a second-half team; are they front runners; which players won't drive (they can be guarded tightly) and which would rather drive than shoot (they can be slacked off); do they have an effective freeze; do they have poise; are they slow getting back on defense; who would be good match-ups for our players on defense; should we play them man-to-man, zone or combination.

• **Conditions Record:** Among the conditions existing on "away" courts that influence the way a team should play its opponent, these are important: size of court; type of nets (does the ball stick thus slowing down the fast break); is the lighting adequate; are the fans close to the floor; what type of backboards are used (glass, wood, fan-shaped); and so on.

We scout the opposing coach. After playing against him for a couple of years you will know how he reacts to a given situation. Is he flexible or does he use the same things year after year? For example, even though he has outstanding shooters on his team, is his zone offense so poor that you might want to use a zone defense anyway? Does he panic or give up when behind? Does he do a poor job fundamentally in preparing his player? We feel that we have won many close games simply because we could tell exactly what an opposing coach was going to do in a certain situation.

We also scout the referees of each game we see and keep a file on each official we face. Most officials have a particularly strong phase of the game and likewise a particularly weak phase.

• **Special Scouting Situations:** On several occasions during each season there are two teams that have to be scouted in one night. In this type of situation, the head coach should go to one game and the assistant the other. It is a good idea, on these split nights, to take one of your players with each of you so that he can keep the shot charts.

One last point concerning scouting that we feel helps us to evaluate our own team is the exchange of scouting reports. We select a coach whose team we don't play during the season—one whose coaching ability we respect—and we scout each other's teams and then exchange reports. As the saying goes, "Sometimes you can't see the forest for all the trees."

4.

GUIDES TO SUCCESSFUL COLLEGE BASKETBALL SCOUTING

by GLEN A. REED

Assistant Basketball Coach
University of Minnesota

After seven years as assistant coach at Minnesota (three under Ossie Cowles and four under John Kundla), Glen Reed became grant-in-aid coordinator, freshman basketball coach, and assistant professor at the University. He is also administrative assistant to the athletic director.

There is nothing a coach would rather do than scout a future opponent himself. Usually, his own team's schedule prevents this, and the job falls to the assistant coach or some friend or associate in a distant town. This means the scout must know what the coach wants, and do the job right.

Here are some guides for coach and scout to get a more effective scouting job done.

1. The Scouting Form. A scouting information form is, simply, a list of questions a scout should be prepared to answer. It is useful even for the assistant coach scouting for his own team (where he is familiar with the head coach and the squad) and invaluable for anyone else doing a scouting job. The scouting form reproduced (Diagram 1) is actually a composite of several such outlines I have received over the years.

BASKETBALL SCOUTING INFORMATION FORM

1. General **comments** on condition, team spirit, coaching techniques, team leader, success to date.

2. Team individual **personnel.** Names, numbers, height, weight, position, experience, personal characteristics, outstanding abilities or weaknesses. This should be for the top 6 or 7 players, including defensive as well as offensive capabilities.

3. Type of **offense** (2-3, 3-2, 1-3-1, etc.):
   a. Position on floor of each player in set attack.
   b. Special out-of-bounds plays (under own basket, side of court).
   c. Special jump ball plays.
   d. Use of fast break and type (dribble, passing, lanes, outlet pass).
   e. Free throw offensive position.
   f. Free throw defensive position.
   g. "Special" offense (high-low pivot, tandem-post, etc.).
   h. Free lance style (how often, by whom).

4. Type of **defense** (man-to-man, zone, switching):
   a. Where the front line lines up in relation to the "head of circle" (extended out court or retreated).
   b. Position of individual defensive players in coverage (who covers on end line, pivot and out court).
   c. Use of the press defense or zone press, and where on court used (full, three-quarter, or half).
   d. Use of "sagging" defense (like zone but pressure on ball by using man-to-man principles with individual responsibility.
   e. How do they defense pivot (front, back or side).

5. Description of offensive **patterns.** Diagram, using:
   > Running
   > Passing
   > Dribbling

6. **Compare** this particular team and its individual to our own, and to squads we have played and know well. General statements that help us to get the "feel" or "pulse" of this new team being scouted.

Diagram 1

The answers to the questions, of course, will go into your written report but you must also know what your coach stresses in scouting and be prepared to answer his "off the cuff" questions when you return.

I have had the pleasure of working for two outstanding basketball coaches at Minnesota—Ossie Cowles and John Kundla—and they both had very different ideas on what to look for and how to present it to the squad.

2. Prepare in Advance: You should prepare for your scouting assignment at least a week in advance, and much of the work can be

16

done right in your office. There is a wealth of material in last year's scouting folder, and this is the big reason for keeping orderly scouting reports in a folder (Diagram 2) from one year to the next.

To be complete, a scouting folder should include all of the information shown in Diagram 2.

In addition, you should discuss the past season's game with the coaching staff, note what players are back this year, and determine in advance what you need to find out about the current team to make a game plan that can result in a victory.

3. Concentrate on Scouting: You have only 40 minutes of playing time to accomplish your mission, so *watch all the action.* Use

Diagram 2

SCOUTING FOLDER CONTENTS

A. Material on game being currently scouted:

    1. Mimeographed report: General comments about opponent.
    (NOTE: Squad receives   Offensive detailed comments.
    copy of this, and is   Defensive detailed comments.
    told about the rest)   Individuals (height, weight, "moves",
        strengths, weaknesses.)
    Statistics of game

    2. Diagrammed plays: Patterns
    Special plays
    Out of bounds plays

    3. Box score: FG-FGA
    FT-FTA
    Rebounds
    Shot charts

    4. Box scores of previous games opponent has played.

    5. Current team and individual statistics.

    6. Report on film from previous year(s) games. (Breakdown by tendencies and give percentage of fast-break, set plays, etc.)

    7. Articles on team from newspapers and magazines. Often posted on bulletin board in locker room)

B. Reference material from previous game or previous year's game:

    1. Last year's report on team.

    2. Last year's game(s) with opponent.

    3. Last year's final statistics of team and individuals.

    4. Last year's game film, if available.

time-outs, half-time, and trips to the foul line for your actual writing, diagramming and note-taking.

You usually won't have time to keep game statistics if you are scouting alone. These are available after the game and in newspaper reports.

Here are some tips to help you get the most out of your time:

- I keep two charts before me that provide ample space for abbreviated notes and diagrams: (a) Sample 1 (Diagram 3) is prepared in advance from information available, and additional material added during the game. You'll probably use two or three of these sheets. (b) Sample 2 (Diagram 4) is a listing of the top six or seven players about whom you will want to make comments as the game progresses, such as favorite moves, defensive reactions, and so on.
- After the game is over, take with you copies of all mimeographed material that is available at the press table, such as statistics, charts, play-by-play and an extra program for the locker-room bulletin board.
- Visit with other scouts at the game. Exchanging information on the game you have just seen can bring you valuable ideas for your report.

You will probably find it difficult to keep shot charts if you are scouting alone. But when you keep them, make sure to label the type of shot (tip, layup, hook, jump, etc.) and mark the exact location on the floor of each shot attempted and scored.

4. Presentation to the Squad: After you have completed your report, discuss it thoroughly with your head coach. One of you will be making the presentation to the squad before going into practice to prepare for that particular opponent. If you make the presentation, follow two simple rules: Be positive and accurate.

Do not build up every opponent in the same manner; each opponent is different and demands a different approach. For example, you cannot build up a weak opponent because this would be inaccurate; yet you cannot scoff at such a team. This is a broad area of coaching psychology and morale; no one can tell you how to handle it.

Two concluding observations: (1) Keep an open mind on new ideas. I have revised my own forms, shot charts and other working

Team Comments

Team Scouted: Ohio State

Opponent: Michigan

Date & Site: Jan. 14th, 1962
                 Columbus, Ohio

▶ Man to man def., #5 on Oosteban

▶ Fast break, Nowell dribble up side, long clear-out pass from #11

▶ Clearout for #3, right side

▶ High Post Continuity (both sides) etc.

▶ Continued team comments on offensive, defense, press, etc.

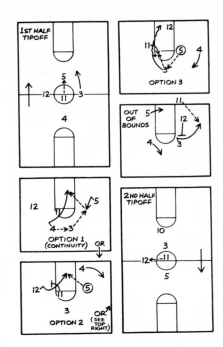

Diagram 3

SCOUTING

INDIVIDUAL COMMENTS (Top 6-7 men)

#5   HAVLICEK, John "Hondo" (F) 6-5, 210 lbs, Sr.—19.1 avg. Second in reb. and scoring. Favors right side. Best def. man. Joins break, often starts it. Overplays men on side. Uses "back door". Goes well without ball. Fair dribbler. Feeds with lob pass. Aggressive, etc.

#12 McDONALD, etc.

Diagram 4

---

materials each year. For example, there is experimenting going on now in the Big Ten (and probably elsewhere) with scouting with the aid of a lightweight portable tape recorder. (2) If you love the game (and you should, if you're coaching it), you'll find scouting is fun. You get the satisfaction of knowing you're doing a very necessary job; you get the pleasure of new associations with coaches, school people, and the press and radio fraternity; and you get the fun of seeing another basketball game.

5.

PREPARING FOR TOURNAMENT PLAY

by MARVIN BECK

Head Basketball Coach
Pensacola Senior (Florida) High School

In 1952, Marvin Beck was a member of Pensacola High School's state championship squad. After playing college ball at Pensacola Junior College and the University of Southern Mississippi, he returned to Pensacola High School in 1956 as assistant basketball coach. He became head coach in 1960. 1964 was Coach Beck's best season—a 25–4 record and the State Class AA championship.

Theoretically, you start preparing for tournament play during pre-season practice. I also feel that all during the season you should have in the back of your mind the thought of playing in a tournament. With positive thinking and a little extra work and planning you have a head start. Here are some of the things we emphasize at Pensacola Senior High School in preparation for tournament play:

• *Grades of Team Members:* A special emphasis is placed on doing a good job in the classroom, particularly the last month before the tournament. Some players we check on all during the year, but we get weekly reports on all varsity players the last month. We encourage players with low marks to bring them up by extra studying after practice. This way those boys can spend more time on basketball before and during the tournament.

• *Health of Players:* We strive to help keep players as healthy as possible. All players get cold shots before the season, and receive vitamin tablets daily. Also, we require short hair so it can be dried thoroughly before leaving the dressing room. Since replacing body salt as soon as possible tends to revive the muscle cells, we have each player take two salt tablets after each practice and especially after a game.

• *Physical Conditioning:* Top physical conditioning is a must for tournament play, so we make definitely certain we meet this requirement. Our conditioning program includes daily work on sit-ups, push-ups, jump rope and jumping drills. We also use weights such as bar bells to develop legs and arms.

We use leg weights in practice until about a week before our first game. After the season has started, we continue to use leg weights the first part of the week only. This gives our boys about two days before the game to adjust to playing without them.

• *Mental Conditioning:* This is one of the most important factors in winning a tournament, or a game. Mental conditioning involves many things. Here are some thoughts on what we feel make for the proper mental frame of mind:

a) Allegiance—All high school boys will give their allegiance to something, and we want this to be the basketball team. This can be accomplished by the coach and the team joining together for one purpose—to win the State Tournament.

b) Knowledge—The more basketball knowledge a player has the easier it will be to develop his morale. Knowledge is gained in practice and games over a period of time, and younger players will develop higher mental spirit and confidence from the knowledge gained from increased practice sessions.

c) Special incentives—You can always use such incentives as trophies and traditions to develop mental readiness. These help to remind your players that others before them have won the tournament and will bring forth special effort.

d) Rest periods—We all learn better if we alternate the working period with a rest period. For example, after working on defense for twenty-five minutes, our rest period is team foul shooting for about five minutes. This also gives us an opportunity to emphasize relaxation in free throw shooting.

• *Offensive Plan:* You must decide which particular phase of your offense you are going to use in tournament play. Naturally, this will be the phase that has been working best for you all year. This is not the time to try new plays. Also, it's important that the players have a say in making up an offensive plan for tournament play, since they will have more confidence in certain plays than others based on past performances.

We prefer keeping the offense simple. While most teams have two offensive systems—one for a zone and one for a man-to-man defense—we run the same basic patterns against both defenses. It works for us. In fact, I think this was an important factor in our winning the state tournament.

For the tournament practice, we never stay on the floor more than one and a half hours. We place special emphasis on speed and quickness. We go back to our offensive fundamentals and try to cover every situation that a game might present.

• *Defensive Plan:* We feel that defense is one of the most important parts of the game, and we coach our players accordingly. Important as scoring yourself, you've got to stop the opponent from scoring. We favor man-to-man defense, and pride ourselves on it being well organized. By this I mean, if we are going to press, each player presses at the same time.

We start our pre-season work with defensive drills for the following reasons: (a) By working on defensive fundamentals first, it helps the players adjust to our thinking that we put defense first in developing a basketball team; (b) There is always a lot of enthusiasm as practice begins and we like to capitalize on this enthusiasm. Psychologists tell us that we learn faster and remember longer the things that are interesting and important to us. So we want that "first impression" for basketball to be defense; (c) All defensive drills are good conditioning drills, and we stress the importance of good physical condition.

In preparing for a tournament, we go back to basic situation drills in defense. We do this because many times you cannot get a good scouting report on teams you are to play. So we feel that if our team is well grounded in the skill of individual man-to-man defense, we can meet and adjust more readily than if any other defense is used.

6.

PUBLIC RELATIONS FOR THE BASKETBALL COACH

by DON PERKINS

Head Basketball Coach
Chapman (California) College

In his seven years as basketball coach at Chapman College, Don Perkins has compiled a 139–50 record; in six of those seven years the Panthers were selected for the NCAA College Division regional tournament, and were runner-up in the 1960 national tournament. In addition, Coach Perkins has guided Chapman to 15 invitational tournament victories in six years. His over-all coaching record to date is 215–138.

Don't kid yourself that winning basketball is just a matter of coaching skills. To be a winner, a coach must have the active support of many people: his players, the faculty, the student body, the opposing team and coaches, the parents, the fans, the alumni, the press and the officials.

When you say "public relations" to the basketball coach, you are talking about all of them. We feel our public relations at Chapman are good; here are some of the things we do.

The Players: A close player-coach relationship is a must for a winner. I feel the toughest hurdle to overcome is the big switch from suitor (recruiter) to disciplinarian (teacher). It's a problem of changing roles.

23

I get some help here, because we don't have the problem of a high pressure recruiting program at Chapman. We recruit, of course, but without a budget for entertaining or campus visits.

I find this technique seems to work: I present our program to the prospective recruit just as if it were at the first squad meeting. I emphasize squad behavior, training rules, and the philosophy of the game as we see it. It gives the boys an advance idea of what we expect.

In addition, I find these two things to be useful:

1. We reserve a half an hour after regular practice for counseling, if needed. Boys come to the coach with personal problems. If the half-hour does not suffice, we set a time the next day for a meeting to continue the discussion.

2. We have a hard and fast rule on trips that players and members of the staff wear jackets and ties. The rule applies on trips to home games, banquets, and so on. While we allow considerable freedom to see points of interest on trips, we try to keep the squad together as much as possible. It builds team spirit.

Married players are common on college teams. To avoid having the wives "left out" of things, we organize a "Wives Club." Mrs. Perkins (an understanding basketball widow) takes charge of this each year. The wives have "pot luck" dinners before each home game, and pool travel accommodations to get to nearby out of town games.

The Faculty and Student Body: Where friction exists between the faculty and the athletic department, I think you'll find it's usually due to lack of communication. We make sure the faculty knows what we are trying to do, and we have no problem. We go a step beyond and try to include the faculty in our athletic programs wherever possible.

Our regular basketball scorekeeper is a full professor of philosophy; our timer is a professor of psychology.

The Opposing Team and Coaches: The visiting team is a guest and should be treated as a guest. We make sure the visiting dressing room is ready when the team arrives. We have a student manager ready to take care of any needs they may have. I make it a policy to meet the opposing coach, confirm the game time and assignment of officials, and see what else he may need. After the game, I make it a point to congratulate the opposing coach on the play of his team.

I feel our players should also congratulate the other team. But this should be a sincere expression of feeling and we do not legislate on this point.

The Parents: True, the high school coach has a far greater responsibility to parents than the college coach, but the college coach cannot overlook them. We work to build up parent support:

- Prior to the season's start, we play a varsity-frosh game, and invite the parents of both teams to attend. After the game, parents are invited to an informal get together in one of the gym rooms. Here we explain our program and meet all parents personally.
- We sponsor a "Dad's Night" during the season. All fathers are invited to a specific game, and both dads and their boys are invited for coffee after the game.

Fans and Alumni: You can't get away from it: the alumni, community groups, high schools and other interested people make great demands on a coach's time—for speeches, presentations, and so on. They usually come during the season, when time is at a premium. There's no help for this; as a coach, you have to give time to it. We feel that, in order to maintain proper rapport with these groups, we must accept as many speaking engagements as possible.

In addition, we do these things:

1. Encourage alumni to come to the locker room after the game to congratulate or commiserate. We don't go over game mistakes at this time. We have an open locker room, to which the press and others (indirectly) are invited.

2. We include alumni and fans in our invitations to the annual awards banquet. We usually give an award to the most loyal fan of the year, determined by vote of the players and coaches.

Candidates might be quite meager in a losing year, but you can usually find a small boy who has followed the team faithfully throughout the year.

The press: In a small school, press relations are vital. Although the main interest of sportswriters is the major colleges, the smaller schools can come in for their share of "ink." To get ours, we do these things:

- Even though it means an 80-mile round trip, we try to get to all Monday luncheons of the Los Angeles Basketball writers.

- We encourage full staff coverage of all games by the local press. I try to call all local papers prior to each home game. Obviously we supply all scores through our news service.
- As already noted, we encourage the press to come to the locker room after each game; or we try to arrange a time for questions directly after the game.
- We hold a "picture day" at the beginning of the season for the press. We invite all papers in the area and turn the entire practice session over to them for the pictures they want.

PART II

OFFENSIVE TECHNIQUES AND DRILLS

1.

DEVELOPING DELIBERATE, DISCIPLINED TEAM OFFENSE

by CHARLES "BUZZ" RIDL

Head Basketball Coach
Westminster (Pennsylvania) College

Buzz Ridl (1962 NAIA Coach of the Year) began coaching at Westminster College, his Alma Mater, in 1949 and became head coach of basketball in 1956. Since 1956, he has compiled a 161–65 record, and in four of the last five years won the NAIA District 30 crown and took his Titans to the Kansas City NAIA tourney. Significantly, since adopting the control game discussed here, Buzz Ridl has a 137–42 record.

Here at Westminster, our offensive philosophy is aimed at playing a controlled game with the objective of shooting only the high percentage shot. We do not believe in using stalling tactics to hold down the score. Every attempt for a lay-up or 10′ shot is made off the first few patterns run. The length of time to accomplish this may be from 15 seconds to two minutes. This depends on our opponent.

We favor the control game for the following reasons:

- All players become a part of the offense and are not bewildered by the expressions or anticipations of one or two players.

29

- We get balanced scoring—a real morale builder. Having all five men average in the double figures really makes each feel a part of the team.
- We don't have to depend on one player's effectiveness for the outcome of our games or our over-all offensive efficiency.
- Contrary to the popular belief that fans and players favor the "run and shoot" game, I have found that we get more compliments from fans after they have watched organized offensive movement.

Here is how we work our offense under our control philosophy:

Diagram 1 shows our basic 3-2 alignment from which we begin our "middle clear through." The most maneuverable jump shooters are the three outside men. Ordinarily, the two inside men are the tallest of the starting five and we prefer a left-hander in the No. 5 spot.

No. 2 may pass either to No. 1 or No. 3. In this diagram, we will follow through with No. 2 passing to No. 3. No. 2 avoids charging his defender as he clears down the middle toward the basket—his speed should be about three-quarters. After the pass and clear, he is encouraged to raise his left arm as if to receive a return pass from No. 3. Nos. 1, 4, and 5 are alerted for the pattern and begin to work on their required positions and assignments. No. 5 works to get open for a pass from No. 3.

In Diagram 2, No. 3 has the ball. He looks to his defensive man and squares off with him on a direct line toward the basket. This makes it easier for him to get the ball to No. 5. If No. 3's defender is a little too strong to the right which might disturb the pass to No. 5, No. 3 should dribble a little to the left before passing. You will also notice that No. 1 and No. 4 have moved into a position to screen No. 2's defender—this screening takes place when No. 2 comes back out from the goal area.

Player No. 5 receives the ball from No. 3 who cuts toward the basket very quickly. (Diagram 3.) He may come close to No. 5 who could use him as a moving screen which would be very convenient for a left-handed dribbler, or he may cut toward the basket within six to eight feet of No. 5. No. 5 now establishes more of a one-on-one situation with his side of the floor cleared for this opportunity. When he catches the ball, he must immediately square

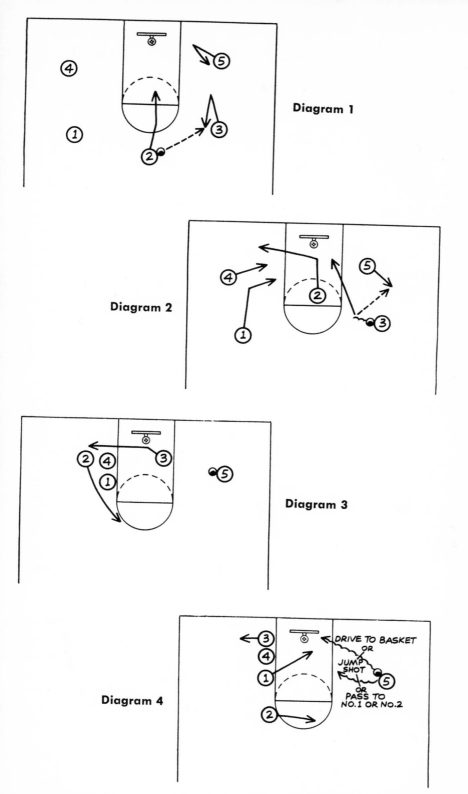

Diagram 1

Diagram 2

Diagram 3

Diagram 4

DRIVE TO BASKET
OR
JUMP
SHOT
OR
PASS TO
NO.1 OR NO.2

off on his defender. This will create the following possibilities: if
his man is sagging, he can take the shot; he can go in for the lay-up;
or he can look for a teammate who may be clear under the basket.
For example, in Diagram 4, we find No. 1 cutting across the lane.
No. 1 must watch, however, to see that No. 5 is not going all the
way before he starts his cut. No. 1 will often get open in this pattern if he watches the head of his defensive man who will, very
often, turn his head to find the ball, or switch out to cover No. 2 at

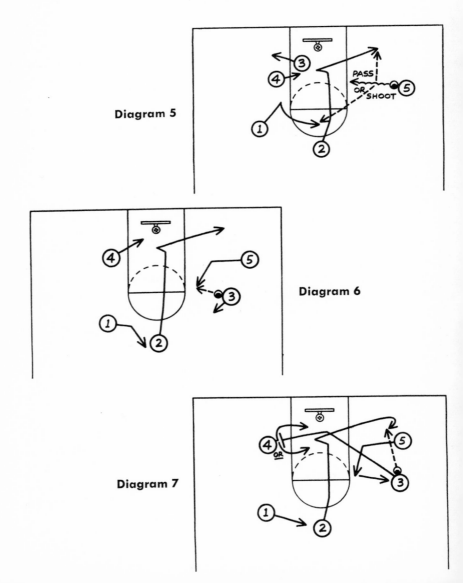

Diagram 5

Diagram 6

Diagram 7

the top of the circle. This is the moment for No. 1 to make his break for an easy goal. If No. 5 does not pass to No. 1, he can toss to No. 2 at the top of the circle who has a high percentage shot, or he can start another cycle to either side.

You will also note that in Diagram 4, No. 3 has established rebounding position because a shot may be taken.

In Diagram 5, the player movement is varied to counteract the defensive floater on No. 2. Some defenders like to short cut No. 2 and not follow around the screens set up by No. 1 and No. 4. Because of this, No. 2 fakes some footwork to the left and breaks to the baseline on the ball-side. This gives him a very nice shot when No. 5 drives to the left toward the foul lane to hit him near the basket. No. 1, who went in to screen for No. 2, notices that he did not come out around his side, and drops back to the top of the circle. No. 1's quick move will often leave him open for a shot. Also, he can come over the top of No. 5's screen for a shot.

The movements illustrated in Diagram 5 are often most effective against zones. The adjustments are very easily adapted. No. 3 may cut through and screen a defender in the area of No. 4. No. 4 may then move to the open spot in the lane.

Other choices would be to have No. 5 slide into the close lane position, while No. 2 slides baseline as shown in Diagram 6. No. 3's first choice should be a pass to No. 5. If No. 5 gets the ball from him, he turns and faces the hoop. He can now shoot, drive or hit No. 2 on the baseline.

No. 5 should also look for No. 4 who has moved to an open spot for a shot. No. 5 may toss over to the weakside to No. 1 who is usually open for a short jumper. No. 3 watches for a clear area to the right or left after he makes his pass to No. 5. In Diagram 6, notice the path of No. 1 to the top of the circle—this is usually taken to receive a pass from No. 3 when he is not able to pass to No. 5. In this case, No. 1 will try to hit No. 5. If No. 1 succeeds in this, all action will be the same as explained in the No. 3 passing to No. 5 action—No. 1 will go down that weakside.

In Diagram 7, No. 3 passes to No. 2. It is an important fundamental for No. 3 to pass to No. 2 only when he has established a shooting position facing the basket—he must not pass if No. 2 is still moving toward the sideline. If this fundamental is followed, No. 2 will be able to shoot as soon as he receives the ball chin high from

No. 3. No. 2 must be aware of the fundamental and make it a point of establishing his shooting position as soon as he can. No. 3 cuts to the basket after passing to No. 2. He does this to get a return pass, a rebound, or to screen a defensive man near No. 4 who will try to take advantage of this screen by looking for an open area. No. 5 then looks for an open area—usually the vacated spot of No. 3. No. 1 should balance out to a defensive position at the top of the key. The move may end with No. 5 getting the ball from No. 2 and then passing out to No. 1 while Nos. 2 and 3 return to the outside to begin the 3-2 attack again.

2.

INDIVIDUAL OFFENSIVE TECHNIQUES

by JOHN E. GALLAGHER

Head Basketball Coach
Scranton (Pennsylvania) Preparatory School

In his 13 years as head basketball coach at Scranton Preparatory School, John Gallagher has coached his teams to a 222–58 record. The tournament record is equally impressive. Gallagher-coached teams have won 9 Diocesan championships, 3 Invitational crowns (3 times runners-up), and were twice state finalists.

Offensive success in basketball hinges on how well players perform in the one-on-one situation. Zone and pattern offenses all aim at getting players into the one-on-one for scoring opportunities. And the team that is well prepared in individual offensive fundamentals is the team that will win its games.

Here at Scranton, we place our greatest coaching emphasis on body balance and footwork—the things so necessary for effective individual offense. Here are the points we stress in our coaching:

STANCE

In order to execute any individual move properly, the player must be in a crouched position at one quarter knee flex. This gives body control which is most important.

35

Efficient movement depends on body control and timing—*not speed*. A crouch position permits rapid execution of the drive, the outside shot, or the pass. It is imperative that the player be made aware of the value of proper stance—knees flexed, tail down, back straight and head up!

FOOT POSITION

We have found that the square position is the most effective for jab and rocker stepping. Both of these moves are designed to get the defensive man into a staggered foot position. Once the defensive man assumes this stance, we work off his front foot. If his left foot is front, our man drives right. If his right foot is front, our man drives left. If the defensive man is in a staggered stance when one of our men receives the ball, we give a head, hip or a shoulder fake and immediately work off his front foot.

The coach *must* tell his players to look at the basket as soon as they receive the ball. This look, combined with a head fake, is one of the best ways to control defense.

LEG POSITION

In order to keep body balance on the jab and rocker steps, the following rules must be observed:

- *Jab Step: (see Figure 1).*
  1. Start from square stance.
  2. Take ¼ to ½ of normal step.
  3. Both knees must be flexed at least ½.
  4. Protect ball by carrying it on hip of leg you're jab stepping with.
  5. When bringing jab leg back, shift weight onto back foot.
  6. Work off the front foot of defensive man if you stagger him.

Figure 1   **Figure 2**

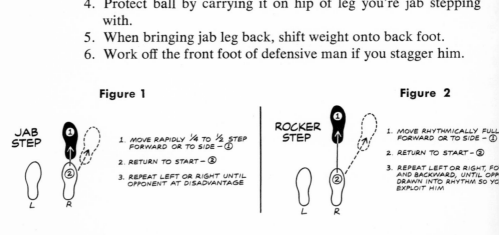

JAB STEP

1. MOVE RAPIDLY ¼ TO ½ STEP FORWARD OR TO SIDE – ①
2. RETURN TO START – ②
3. REPEAT LEFT OR RIGHT UNTIL OPPONENT AT DISADVANTAGE

ROCKER STEP

1. MOVE RHYTHMICALLY FULL FORWARD OR TO SIDE – ①
2. RETURN TO START – ②
3. REPEAT LEFT OR RIGHT, FO AND BACKWARD, UNTIL OPP DRAWN INTO RHYTHM SO YO EXPLOIT HIM

If the defensive man does not react to cover the side you are jab stepping to, drive right off that step. If he does react, bring jab leg back and drive off the opposite jab step.

- *Rocker Step:* (*see Figure 2.*)
  1. Start from square stance.
  2. Take full stride.
  3. Protect ball by carrying it on the hip on side of rocker leg.
  4. When returning rocker leg to original square stance, make sure that both knees are flexed as they were when you started.
  5. Remember to use the head fake and look at the basket. The reaction of defense will determine what can be done. If you force defense into staggered stance, work off the front foot.
  6. By taking a rocker step forward, recovering to original position and then taking a rocker step backward, you can force defensive man into a position that can be exploited by a drive or an outside shot.
  7. You can get your defensive man into a rhythm by rocker stepping forward and backward. When he is in this rhythm, he is susceptible to both the drive and the outside shot—the drive when he moves toward you, and the outside shot when he moves away. Concentrate on head and shoulder fakes with this move and keep the ball in position to get the outside shot (set or jump) off without time loss.

BALL RECEPTION

In order to execute *any* individual offensive move effectively, it is vital to have excellent reception of the ball. A juggle, fumble or dropped pass will kill any play. Here are the coaching points we make sure our boys understand about passing:

1. Keep your eyes on the ball at all times. Know where the ball is when you cut by glancing over your shoulder.
2. Meet the ball every time it is passed to you and continue toward it until contact is made.
3. The hands and the ball should be going in the same direction at the time of reception. As the ball makes contact with the hands, the hands should give to receive ball—this is *reception*. If the hands and the ball are going in different directions, you have *resistance* which results in errors.

FIND THE "OPEN MAN"

Any time a defensive man tries to help a teammate, we put our "find the open man" rule into effect. The offensive man of the helper cuts to the basket and yells for the ball. The man with the ball must be alert for this situation and get the ball to the open man quickly.

There are two bad habits that take away from a player's alertness: (1) Looking at the floor when faking; and (2) Looking at the floor when dribbling. They can be corrected by the use of dribbling blinders and dribbling obstacle drills.

3.

INDIVIDUAL OFFENSIVE MANEUVERS

by Joseph W. Hartley

Assistant Basketball Coach
Northern Illinois (DeKalb) University

Joseph W. Hartley coached varsity basketball for 24 years in Illinois high schools. His lifetime coaching record is .600, and includes 12 tournament championships and 6 conference championships. At present, he is assistant basketball coach at Northern Illinois University.

Many fine shooters in high school basketball are limited by their inability to maneuver for openings once a defensive player has them clamped. A player may be the finest shot in the game when he is open; but if he lacks the knowledge of how to maneuver to get open once the defense is on him, he's just another average player unable to take advantage of his shooting prowess.

First, of course, a boy must be taught to shoot, if he isn't a good shot to begin with. Next, to become a consistent scorer of polish and class, he must be taught individual maneuvers that will free him against the various defenses he will encounter.

Most of the individual maneuvers we teach are based on the moves that a player will make when he has the ball. Our premise is that any boy, to be a better than average player, must (1) shoot a fair percentage from the outside, and (2) be able to drive. Toward that end, we stress the following offensive maneuvers:

Rocker Step: Give the boy a ball and put a defensive man on him. Have the player with the ball just rock back and forth against the defensive man, or step at him and then step as far back from him as possible. This way he'll get the feeling of moving against the defensive man. If at any time the defensive man moves at the ball or with the offensive player—the offense should burst by him with a driving dribble.

From the above move, the offense should be taught the following fakes (1) fake a shot—drive; (2) fake a drive—shoot. The offense now has the basic foundation for other individual maneuvers.

Walking Step: Next we stress the walking step or hesitation step from the rocker movement. In this movement the player, after taking a step forward, and then backward, takes a hesitation step of about half-a-step length forward, then bursts on by the defensive man with a driving dribble. The hesitation, followed by the burst of speed, makes for a surprise move that will prove successful.

Cross-over Step: On the cross-over step from the rocker movement, the player with the ball takes a jab-step (half a step) quickly toward the defensive man—then a cross-over step and goes hard by the defensive man for the basket.

Lead Step: A lead step is a move with the near foot in the direction you are going. If going to the left, you lead off with the left, and vice versa. The cross-over, on the other hand, is a move whereby you step with the far foot in the direction you are going. An example would be stepping with the left foot across the body to the right. This is a good move to make after faking a drive with a lead step left, then crossing-over going to the right.

In addition to the above steps, we have certain other movements we want all players to master from both the forward operational areas and the pivot post area. Some of these follow:

Forward Area: Our forwards start their moves from the position shown in Diagram 1. The player faces the inside or toward the middle taking a position about two strides from the side line and about three steps back of the free-throw line. This enables him to see the movements of all his teammates as well as those of his opponents, and should also enable him to free himself from the defense to receive a pass without ever being any further toward the center of the floor than the free-throw line extended.

Before our forwards move out to receive the ball from the guards

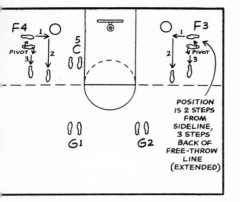

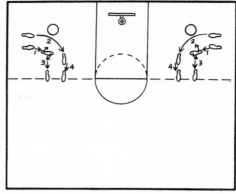

Diagram 1   **Diagram 2**

—if the defense is playing them close or in such a way that there's danger of interception—we stress "shaking the defensive man" with a move toward him on the *near foot* in a lead step, faking a drive then stepping out to receive the ball (Diagram 1). If this does not free him, we try stepping at the defensive man with the *far foot* —throwing the body in front of the defense by a following step on the *inside foot* and moving out to receive the ball from the guard in a well protected position (Diagram 2).

Individual Moves: When the forward receives the ball, he will have his back to the defensive man. From this position, here are some of the individual moves we teach our forwards to make:

1. *Front turn drive:* This may be made on either the inside or the outside foot by stepping across the pivot foot with the opposite foot. In making the front turn drive, the player executes the pivot, takes a full lead step and takes off on the drive in the desired direction. In doing this, the player knows that he is open and that no faking is desired.

2. *Front turn cross-over drive:* This move is usually made on the inside foot. The player steps across the pivot foot with the opposite foot. But instead of taking a full lead step, only a half step is taken on the front turn and from this a cross-over step is made. The player explodes in a drive as the ball is dropped forward and to the outside for protection as the driving dribble is started.

From the front turn executed in the forward position, or in any other position, any of the "rocker series" of movements may be made. They blend in well with the movements just described.

3. *Reverse pivot drive:* This is made by stepping backwards with the foot opposite the pivot foot, so as to execute a half turn of the

41

body, facing the opposite direction from that when the movement was started. When desired and when advantageous to do so, a three-fourths or a quarter-turn of the body may be made. As with the front turn, we usually turn or pivot on the inside foot (but the pivot may be made to advantage at times on the outside foot). From the pivot, a lead step drive or a cross-over step drive may be executed.

4. *Front turn:* In this move the defense plays the forward loosely so that he has no trouble receiving the ball. Thus, no "shaking" or "faking" movements are necessary. In this situation, we tell our forward to move out to receive the ball with the outside foot and leg forward. He would then receive the ball on the outside shoulder and be almost facing his opponent. The forward turns on the balls of his feet as he receives the ball, so as to bring his body facing toward the base line or toward the basket. He follows with a lead step on the foot nearest the base line—at the same time dropping the ball in front of the lead foot and pushing off on the back foot— dashing by the defensive man with a driving dribble toward the base line and the basket. Diagram 3 illustrates the footwork for this move.

A player can make all of the above moves without the ball as well as with it. In fact, in such a case, a player can reverse quicker and maneuver faster. Make sure your boys are aware of this and use these movements to get open when maneuvering without the ball.

Pivot Post Area: We teach these same maneuvers for execution within the pivot post area—that is, from the top of the free-throw circle to the base line, and along the sides of the free-throw lanes. In this area, we refer to the maneuvers as the "spinner series," but the movements are essentially the same as when executed from the forward positions.

With our pivot players and in the pivot post area, we put added emphasis upon another maneuver which we call the "inside pivot." This is a move by the player with the ball in the pivot post area to get the opponent on his inside hip or the hip nearest the opponent —and to give the shooter the advantage of a step away from or by his opponent. This, when combined with a hook shot, can be deadly and can also at times give the shooter a shot close enough that he need not hook.

The maneuver is little more than a reverse pivot on the foot next to the opponent. It can be executed in any number of positions

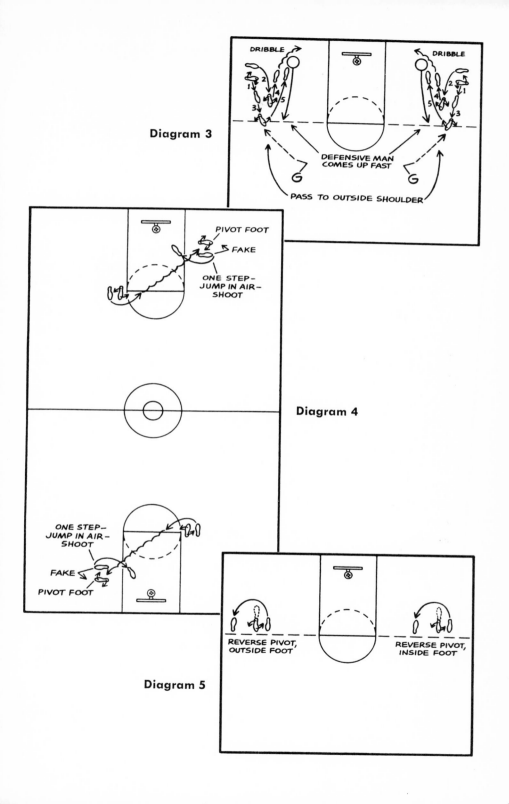

Diagram 3

DRIBBLE

DRIBBLE

DEFENSIVE MAN
COMES UP FAST

G

G

PASS TO OUTSIDE SHOULDER

PIVOT FOOT

FAKE

ONE STEP—
JUMP IN AIR—
SHOOT

Diagram 4

ONE STEP—
JUMP IN AIR—
SHOOT

FAKE

PIVOT FOOT

REVERSE PIVOT,
OUTSIDE FOOT

REVERSE PIVOT,
INSIDE FOOT

Diagram 5

in and around the pivot post area. All that's required is that the offensive player get his defensive opponent moving with him. Once the offense gets his opponent moving with him and sees no clear drive by him, the offense stops, plants both feet and, if necessary, fakes a shot. Any declaration on the part of the defense should enable the offensive player to execute the pivot on the foot nearest the defensive player—stepping backward and toward the basket, thereby placing his opponent on his hip in such a manner as to cleverly spin by him and get an almost unmolested shot. Diagrams 4 and 5 illustrate this move.

This maneuver can be made anywhere in the pivot post area, or within a 12 to 14 foot area of the basket. Some players with a long step and a float through the air can cover an amazing distance with this move.

4.

SIMPLE
PATTERN OFFENSE

by GENE STAUFFER

Head Basketball Coach
Salina (Kansas) High School

In the 1963 Kansas state championship finals, Coach Gene Stauffer's Salina team faced Wyandotte, of Kansas City, a team with a 22–0 record and a background of 5 state championships and 2 second-place finishes in 7 years. Salina won, and the state championship climaxed Gene Stauffer's four-year rebuilding program and made Salina's two-year record 35–9.

I've learned this: If a coach attempts to teach high school players the complete offensive system he was taught and played at college, more often than not the high school players will find the many patterns and options more than they can handle. The boys become so involved with timing, cuts, passes, picks, and so on that they forget the object of the game is to put two points on the board.

A high school coach must face facts. One fact is that he cannot spend the entire season teaching an intricate set offense with options off each pattern.

Of course, an offense that is easy to teach and understand is only part of the story; it has to be good enough to win games. In developing our offense, we wanted one that would work equally well

45

against the various zone and man-to-man defenses thrown against us, and above all, one that would give us the high percentage shot with good rebound power.

Our simple pattern offense does all this. Here is what it is and how we man it; the rules that govern our play; and how it works. We made very few adjustments for the defense. A zone and man-to-man were attacked in very nearly the same manner.

• *Player No. 1* is the point position. Since he starts the offense, he must be the best playmaker. We *like* to have the ball in possession of the point man when he is still in the back court area. *Definitely,* by the time he crosses the mid-court line, the point man must be in control of the ball.

Our offense consists of a point man, two wing men, and a double post (Diagram 1).

• *Players No. 2 and 3* are the wing men. They should be good set or preferably jump shooters, and be tough rebounders. They must be able to fake and drive from the one-on-one situation. The wing men must hustle to position, size up the defense, and free themselves for a possible pass from the point position.

• *Players No. 4 and 5* are the double post. Normally, they are the tallest, most talented, and most aggressive players. Timing between the post players is such that when at all possible they receive the pass from the point or wing men while stepping or on the move toward the ball or basket.

The post men should always be the best rebounders and be in position for the second or third shot, or tip-in.

On the fast break, we box out on defense and rebound with all five men, if possible. Dribbling is a last resort to get the ball down court. We fill the lanes on a first-come, first-served basis and have one trailer down the middle. If we are in a good position for

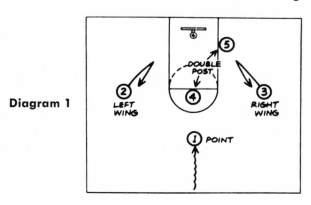

Diagram 1

the short jump shot or can drive all the way, we take the shot. The shot is taken only if we are equal to, or outnumber, the defense.

When we cannot get the good shot, we immediately move the ball out to the point position, and start our offense.

We attempt to follow these rules that pertain to all three options off our double post:

1. The post players determine what option to use.
2. The defense will help decide what options are best.
3. The point man may hit the double post directly, pass to either wing man, fake and drive, or look for the outside shot. A great deal of freedom must be given the point player; he is the defensive balance.
4. Wing men, after receiving the pass, immediately pivot and face the basket. The defense will name the next move.
5. Double post players execute their moves to be in position when the wing men, or the point man, are ready to work to them.
6. Always look for an open man when starting a fake and drive.
7. Get the closest and best shot to the basket on every move.
8. Always go back up for the shot when under the basket— draw the foul.
9. Get a second and third shot by aggressive rebounding on any missed shot.
10. Do not force the offense. Move the ball back out of trouble and start over.

Simple Pattern Options: Our offense consists of just three options off the double post. In the explanation below of each option, I have kept things simple by starting each from the left wing (No. 2) position.

First is our *high-low double post attack* (Diagram 2). When No. 1 sees No. 4 on the free-throw line, he is ready to key the next move. No. 1 passes to No. 2 and fakes through to the baseline on the strong side. No. 3 may become the defensive balance or weak side rebounder, replacing No. 1, depending on whether a shot is taken. No. 2, after facing in to the basket, looks for No. 4 or No. 5 on the double post. If neither is open, No. 2 looks to No. 1 on the baseline. Should No. 2 pass to No. 1, No. 2 goes for the basket. Then,

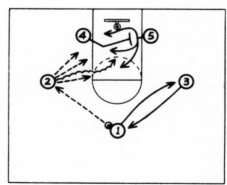

Diagram 2

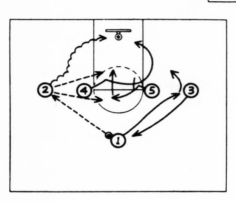

Diagram 3

Diagram 4

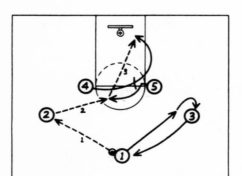

Diagram 5

if he does not receive the ball (or No 1 does not have a shot), No. 2 moves out to the point position and the continuity starts again.

Second is our *double high post option* (Diagram 3). No. 1 passes to No. 2. After the pass, No. 1 exchanges with No. 3 on the weak side. No. 2 faces in to the basket and looks for No. 5 coming across the lane. If No. 5 is not open, No. 2 fakes and drives to the baseline, looking for a pass to No. 4 under the basket. If the pass goes from No. 2 to No. 5, No. 5 will look for a shot or pass to No. 4 under the basket. (Another possibility is that No. 5 may pass to No. 1 on the weak side. If an opportunity to score does not materialize, the ball is passed to the point position to start the same or another option.)

Third is the *double low post option* (Diagram 4). No. 1 passes to No. 2. After the pass, No. 1 exchanges with No. 3. No. 2 looks for No. 5 coming across the lane for a pass. If No. 5 receives the ball, he looks for the shot or possible pass to No. 4 under the basket. If No. 5 is not open, No. 2 has the option of faking and driving to the middle, again always looking for an open man. No. 2, when stymied, has either No. 3 or No. 1 as an outlet to start the continuity for the same or different option.

The defense, of course, will determine what move will be necessary. The only adjustments made will be if the defense is man-to-man; then a good legal pick or screen must be set, requiring the defense to check or switch. The check or switch is usually the most difficult maneuver for the defense to make consistently.

When the wing man or point man passes to either double post man, the first move for the post man is to look for the other post man. This is especially true if the team has a high-scoring post man —he draws the defense like flies and allows the other member of the double post to roost under the basket, wide open in many cases.

Delay Game: We found another use for our simple pattern offense: as a delay game. By spreading the wing men out from the top of the circle, moving the point man into a double high post, we were able to delay, plus score off the lay-in (Diagram 5).

5.

"LANE"
OFFENSIVE PATTERNS

by GALEN KINTNER

Head Basketball Coach
Catalina (Tuscon, Arizona) High School

After serving three years as JV basketball coach (record: 42–9) at Catalina High School, Galen Kintner took over as head coach at the start of the 1962–63 season. In his first year, he went all the way to the state championship with a 20–2 record. He's been doing equally well ever since.

Every year we teach at least three offenses, in addition to the fast break and stall game. I firmly believe that the boys can learn these things and my teams have demonstrated that ability.

I believe in changing offensive patterns from time to time, not necessarily because I think the new variation is better but because I want to give the team some new incentive or added interest.

After all, there are certain basics or fundamentals and these can be transferred to different offensive or defensive patterns or assignments. My philosophy of basketball is probably not much different from many other coaches, but here are a few basic points of mine:

1. With the exception of the lay-up shot, we insist on rebounding being available upon all shots in any type of offense we are running.
2. We seldom pass the ball more than twice, or have more than

one man dribble before shooting; we do not use a pattern offense that has continuity as most coaches know continuity.

3. Our boys do not play different positions. Our guards are always out, our forwards always in, and our center or pivot man plays near the free throw line.

4. If we are stopped from shooting or driving for the basket, we coach our boys to pass immediately to our back-up man. He then starts something else.

5. We try, and usually have, a back-up man in all situations. He is also our back man to prevent the cheap basket by the opposition.

In our championship year, we were a controlled fast-break club; we broke only when we had, or were going to have, an advantage. When we set up on offense, we used a "gang" or "lane" offensive pattern most of the time. The thing that made our offense "go" was that the defensive men were moving, because our men without the ball had assignments that made them part of the total offense, even if they were not going to shoot, or even handle the ball, in a particular situation.

I am sold on this type of offense with either three or four men near the lane because we get good shots anywhere from 6 to 18 feet out, and have rebounders in, or moving in, to position. Also, we have one man back, and usually a second in position to recover quickly and play defense. During the championship season, only one fast-break basket was scored on us.

We set up as shown in Diagram 1. From this set-up, here are three offensive patterns that worked well for us:

1. O-1 has the ball and starts his drive for the basket trying to get a lay-up or short jumper. If he is stopped by the defense, he passes back to O-2 who backs him up. O-2 will try a pass to O-3 who has cut off the screens set by O-4 and O-5. O-4 and O-5 are rebounders with O-3 covering his own shot in the lane. (Diagram 2.)

2. O-2 starts by dribbling toward O-1's defensive man. He hands back to O-1 who dribbles toward the left side of the lane, and if he does not shoot, he passes to O-3 along the end line. O-4 and O-5 are the rebounders, with O-2 going to the free-throw line after he hands off to O-1. (Diagram 3.) This play is simple, but it works and gets results for us.

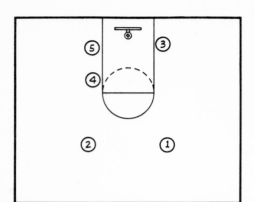

Diagram 1

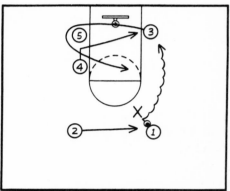

Diagram 2

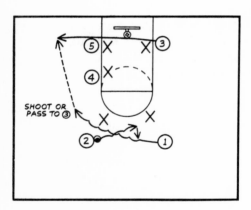

Diagram 3

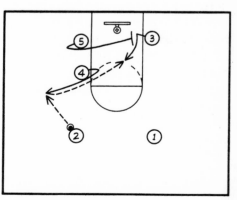

Diagram 4

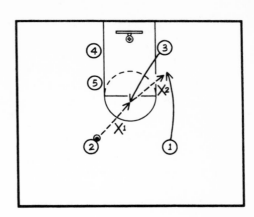

Diagram 5

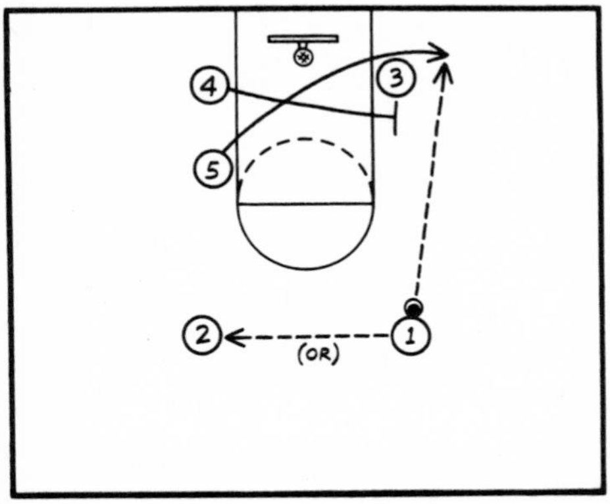

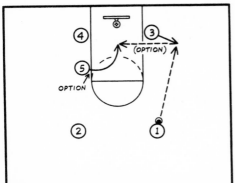

Diagram 6

Diagram 7

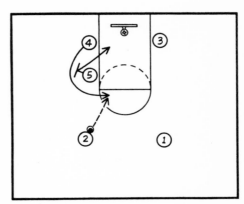

Diagram 8

53

3. O-2 passes to O-4 breaking out, after faking his guard in. O-4 is to try to maneuver so as to get the drive or jumper off his defensive man. If O-5 sees that O-4 can do neither, he screens for O-3 and O-4 passes to O-3 in the lane. O-4 rebounds on the left side; O-5 on the right side; and O-3 rebounds in the lane. (Diagram 4.)

We vary our basic offensive set-up by having the front post man line up on either side of the lane; we can run our options on either side and make it harder on the defense. And, as shown in the special plays that follow, we also use our inside men to screen for each other.

4. We scored an average of three baskets a game on this one: O-3 fakes his man in and breaks to the right half of the free-throw line. He receives a pass, usually a bounce pass, from O-2. At the same time, O-1 breaks by his man and receives the pass from O-3. (Diagram 5.) The key to this play is to study the defense to see when you can break.

5. This play gives us options to keep the defense honest: O-4 moves alongside of O-3 to set a double screen for O-5, who breaks along the end line for a pass from O-1. If O-5 does not get open, O-1 passes to O-2 who has the whole left side of the floor to work a one-on-one situation. (Diagram 6.)

6. O-4 fakes in, swings up around O-5 for a pass from O-2. He must go as close to O-5 as possible so O-5 can set an inside screen on O-4's defensive man. O-4 either gets his jump shot near the free-throw line, or if he is picked up by O-5's defensive man he looks for O-5 who should have the inside position on his new defensive man (formerly guarding O-4) as he rolls to the basket. (Diagram 7.)

7. This play utilized the abilities of our O-3 man, who was a very good player. We let him break out a short distance from the lane for a pass from O-1. He was then to work his defensive man in a one-on-one situation. If he did not get his jump shot or drive by the count of three, O-5 tried to get the inside position on his defensive man and break down the lane for a pass from O-3. (Diagram 8.)

6.

THE 3-2
FREE LANCE OFFENSE

by Rudy Yaksich

Head Basketball Coach
Brilliant (Ohio) High School

*Building a winner from the ground up is not just a phrase
with Coach Rudy Yaksich. Look at the four-year record at
Adena (Ohio) High School: 2–16 (1959–60); 9–9 (1960–
61); 10 8 (1961–62); 21–5 (1962–63). The 1962 63 team
(the second year for his free-lance offense) won the league,
sectional and district championships. At present, Rudy Yaksich is head basketball coach at Brilliant High School.*

There are a number of reasons why I feel our 3-2 free-lance
offense has advantages for the high school team: It is simple to
learn, maintains floor balance, can be used against both a zone and
man-to-man defense, and keeps us in good rebounding positions.
But the first reason is the most important: It is based entirely on
the execution of fundamental basketball moves.

This being true, it follows that all moves, fakes and screens must
be executed to perfection if they are to work satisfactorily. In coaching, we emphasize this and permit no mediocre screens and rolls.

In this article, I will give you the basic positioning and moves in
our offense, a few illustrative offensive patterns, and an idea of our
drill schedule to perfect our boys in the basic moves.

1. Positioning and Moves: Diagram 1 shows our basic alignment for the 3-2 free lance. O-1 is the quarterback; he sets up the offense by passing to either O-2 or O-3. He must be a good jump shooter and driver. O-2 and O-3 are outside shooters and drivers, capable of making all the fundamental moves. They play two to three feet from the sideline, in order to keep the middle open for screens or rolls to the basket. O-4 and O-5 are mainly concerned with rebounding; they must be able to maneuver in the pivot and set back screens on O-2 and O-3.

The first step in developing the offense is to work on the basic moves until they become second nature to the players. Diagrams 2 through 9 show you these moves. Our players execute them and call

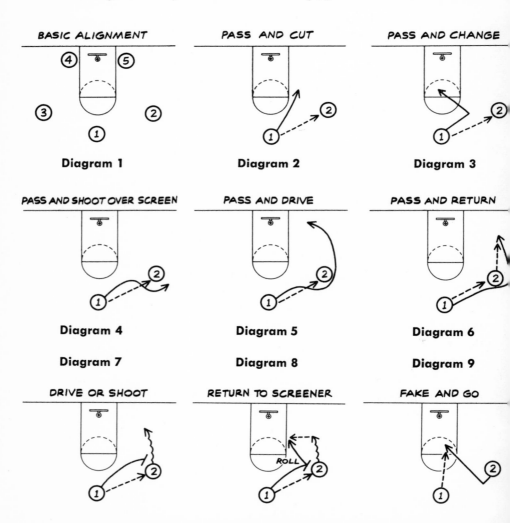

| BASIC ALIGNMENT | PASS AND CUT | PASS AND CHANGE |
| Diagram 1 | Diagram 2 | Diagram 3 |

| PASS AND SHOOT OVER SCREEN | PASS AND DRIVE | PASS AND RETURN |
| Diagram 4 | Diagram 5 | Diagram 6 |

| Diagram 7 | Diagram 8 | Diagram 9 |

| DRIVE OR SHOOT | RETURN TO SCREENER | FAKE AND GO |

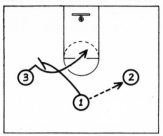

SCREEN OPPOSITE GUARD

Diagram 10

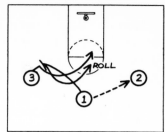

SCREEN AND ROLL

Diagram 11

them out by name. (These are to the right; identical moves are made to the left.) This takes up 40 minutes of our practice time each day (see schedule). I emphasize again: The moves must be made with precision.

When O-1, O-2, and O-3 have learned these two-man moves, we add the third man to the offense, which adds two more basic moves which must be perfected.

- Diagram 10 shows the use of the opposite screen; it involves the same basic moves by O-1 and O-3, but with the ball on the opposite side of the court.
- Diagram 11 shows an extension of the same move, with the screener (O-1) using a roll after O-3 breaks for the basket.

When these moves have been perfected, we add a defense to the drills. We use five defensive men, which makes the offense set their picks and rolls to perfection if they are to free themselves. This three-on-five situation emphasizes the need for accurate passing as well as receiving.

We then give more movement to our offensive drills by adding O-4 and O-5. Although these two men are primarily concerned with rebounding, they do have offensive moves in our attack:

- Diagram 12 shows the back screen option. O-1 passes to O-2, whose defensive man is screened by O-5. O-2 dribbles toward the basket; he has the option of driving all the way or passing to O-5 who rolls toward the basket after the back screen. After any screen, O-4 and O-5 must automatically roll toward the basket; this puts them in rebound territory and in position for the return pass.

57

• Diagram 13 shows the option of breaking toward the post at any opportune time and receiving a pass. When this is done, and any guard passes to O-5 in the post, a split is made by the passer and O-1.

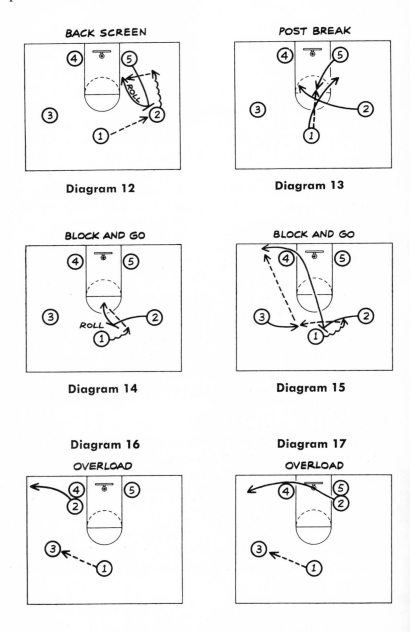

BACK SCREEN

Diagram 12

POST BREAK

Diagram 13

BLOCK AND GO

Diagram 14

BLOCK AND GO

Diagram 15

Diagram 16

OVERLOAD

Diagram 17

OVERLOAD

Through experience, players in the O-1, O-2 and O-3 positions should be able to execute the moves from any one of the three positions. This is particularly helpful against high school man-to-man defenses; many defensive players are accustomed to having their offensive opponent play in one position and tend to fall into that area rather than looking for their man.

Although we call out our moves in practice, we do not do so in game conditions. By repeated practice of these moves against defense and by studying one's specific defensive man in man-to-man situations, the players soon learn what can and cannot be used. Also, on the basis of scouting reports, we can specify what moves and series will be more effective.

2. *Offensive Patterns:* Here are a few offensive patterns in our offense:

- Against a zone: The key is to move the ball quickly to keep the defense out of position; we try to do this without using any definite pattern at first. We do have certain moves. In one option (Diagram 14) we rotate the ball around the outside quickly for the outside shot. O-3 blocks for O-1 and rolls through. O-1 drives off the block and may jump or pass to O-3 cutting. O-4 keeps his man occupied; O-5 cuts out slightly to corner for the potential pass, and O-2 rolls to back of circle.
- *Overload #1:* Another option, or overload (Diagram 15), is the same as Diagram 1 except that O-3 passes to O-2 at the top of the circle. O-2 passes to O-3 who cuts to weak side after coming around weak side baseline block.

In play, we find that many of our basic man-to-man moves will work against the zone and we use them.

- *Overload #2:* In a set up as shown in Diagram 16, O-1 passes to O12; as the pass is made, O-3 cuts to the corner. O-2 has the following options: (a) pass to O-3; (b) take a shot himself; (c) hit O-4 under the basket; or (d) return the ball to O-1 who can hit O-5 breaking out. The same move can be made with O-3 setting up on the opposite side just to keep the defense honest (Diagram 17).

3. *Practice Schedule:* Our individual practice schedules follow. We allow 40 minutes per day to these individual drills.

Forwards and Centers

Drill	Station	Amount	Comments
Rebound machine	1	50	Start at average height; increase jumping height each day. Manager keeps height record.
Tipping right	2	50	Use both one-hand jab and two-hand tip. Meet the ball as it starts downward.
Tipping left	3	50	Same.
Rebound "blast up" right	4	50	Grasp ball and protect it with the body; jump high and hard and lay the ball off the board.
Rebound "blast up" left	5	50	Same.
Jumping chair	6	50	Work on increasing jumping ability. Bend knees when landing.
Medicine ball	7	25	Lying flat on the floor throw the ball to your partner.
Ball grasping	8	50	Throw ball in the air, jump high and "jerk" it out of the air.

Alternate Plan

Drill	Station	Amount	Comments
Hooks, rear in, Jump shot right	2	50	Work on the shot underneath as if in a game situation.
Jump shot left	3	50	Be graceful in your moves.
Jump rope	7	50	Both feet.
		25	Each foot. (Work on rhythm in movement.)
Tipping wall	8	50	Control ball with both hands; try to do 50 in succession.

Guards

Drill	Time	Comments
Jump shooting from favorite spot	10 min.	Work on the shots you will get in game situations.
Jump shooting from five floor areas	10 min.	These are the areas you will be shooting from in game situations. Shoot as if it was in a game.
Basic moves off the free lance offense	10 min.	Start with two, and add the third man. Make sure the cuts, fakes, and especially the picks and rolls, are done correctly.
Free lance patterns by guards against zone defense	10 min.	Move ball quickly around the outside; make sure men are facing basket upon receiving the ball.

7.

THE CONTROL FAST BREAK

by CHUCK MUNDELL

Head Basketball Coach
Centralia (Illinois) Junior College

Which was the USA's top scoring basketball team in 1962–63? Chuck Mundell's Centralia Junior College squad with a 98.4 per game average. It was no flash in the pan; they did it again in the 1963–64 season (117.0 pts. per game)— and again in the 1964–65 season (109.0 pts. per game). In 11 years at Centralia, Coach Mundell has won the conference championship 8 times, has been in the top 12 in junior college scoring 4 times, and has compiled a 184–91 record.

Too many fast break teams know only one thing—running; they concentrate on the fast break at the expense of team play and defense. We are a fast break team at Centralia—I feel it works best in developing the talents of the two-year junior college player—but appreciate possession of the ball. We let go of the ball only when we have a *better* than 50–50 chance of scoring. The philosophy works under game conditions: in the past three years, our scoring percentage from the field has been 46%.

FAST BREAK STARTING POINTS

We will attempt the fast break from all possible starting points.

62

We feel this constant threat makes the opponent anxious on offense and worried about getting back on defense. Here are the situations in which we can attempt the fast break:

• *Defensive Rebounds:* The quick pass-out from under-the-basket traffic is the key to the success of the fast break. If we do not get it out fast, then we slow down for a pattern offense. To get the rebounds, each player turns and blocks out his opponent and we try to move in with a rebounding triangle, composed of the pivot man and two forwards. Our guards move into the circle to play the high bouncing rebounds (Diagram 1).

We sometimes rebound by the use of the cross block. The three inside men move in front of the opposite men, especially on the offensive board where we may be blocked out (Diagram 2).

• *Controlled Tip:* If we feel sure we can control a jump ball (at mid-court or defensive court), we line up with the two forwards on the offensive side of the circle and our two guards on the defensive side. We start the move by having G-1, the guard in back of our tipper, break around to the side we intend to tip to. F-1 (we do not tip to him) is sent back to steal or help on defense in the event we don't get the tip. G-2 drops back on defense. If we do get the tip, we fill the three lanes and go on our fast break (Diagram 3).

• *Full-Court Press:* Against a full-court press, we try to get the ball to mid-court fast and outnumber the back court before the down-court pressers can get back to defense. We line up with our forwards and our pivot man across the center of the floor at mid-court (Diagram 4). One guard, G-1, takes the ball out and the other guard, G-2, breaks toward the ball. If we get the ball in to G-2, he passes up court to either F-1 or C (whichever is open), and we go down on a three-lane fast-break attempt. If we can't get the ball to G-2, the two forwards break toward the ball. If we hit one of them, he will pass off to the pivot man and we will go down in three lanes. If one of the forwards does not get the ball, the pivot will cut toward the defensive foul line and we will try to hit him with a pass. If we do, we go on the fast break in three lanes. This is a rough play to perfect. It is hard to get the ball in bounds within 5 seconds—it can be done—but takes practice.

• *Scored Goal:* Several times during a game on a scored goal, we will have an inside man take the ball out of the net, step back and

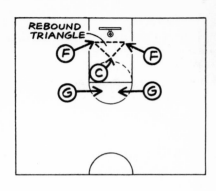

Diagram 1

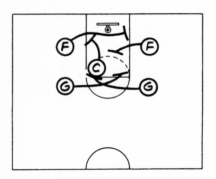

Diagram 2

Diagram 3

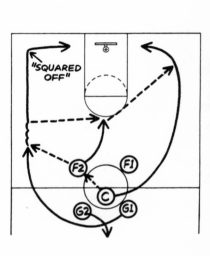

Diagram 4

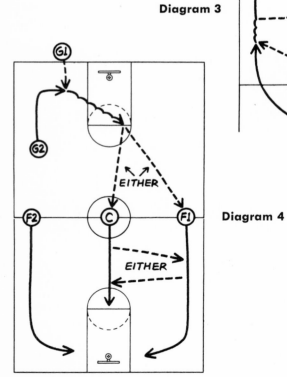

fire the ball up court. We will try this more often against a zone defense team.

SPREAD RULES

Before we discuss actual fast break situations and how we work them at Centralia, it is necessary to explain our "spread rules." These rules are used on any ratio situation (one-on-one, two-on-one, etc.). Here is what we tell our boys:

A. Keep spread and do not bunch up. Reason: if two men come in toward the basket close together, then one defensive man can take care of them.

B. When coming down court, cut all corners square (see the diagrams) about five feet from the baseline and three feet from the sideline. Don't round off so that the outside men are too close to the center man.

C. On the three-on-two, if the ball ends up with the center man, he should stop at the foul line and make the defense commit itself (either drop back or come forward). If they drop back, the center man takes a jumper from the foul line. If they come out to cover, the center man tries to feed off an open man under the basket.

D. If we end up with the ball on the side, we use the same commit principle—the man with the ball stops six to eight feet from the basket along the baseline and makes the defense commit itself. He then either shoots the jumper or feeds off.

FAST BREAK SITUATIONS

Here are the fast break situations and how we work them:

1. *One-on-none:* This happens infrequently. We break fast on an intercepted pass or on occasion send a guard down as a "sleeper" and try to hit him with a baseball pass.

2. *Two-on-one:* (Intercepted pass, travel violation, or high rebound.) Our two men spread out and try to get the defense to commit himself to one of them. They then proceed according to the "spread rules" (Diagram 5).

3. *Three-on-two:* (Defensive rebound or pass after score.) This is a common situation. We spread the defense by having the man with

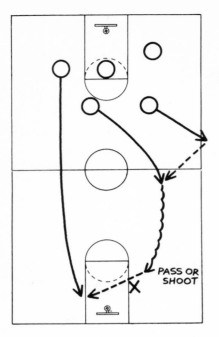

Diagram 5

PASS OR
SHOOT

X

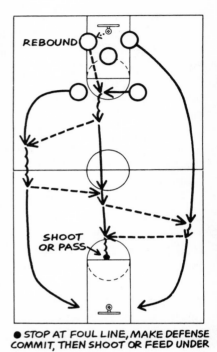

REBOUND

SHOOT
OR PASS

Diagram 6

● STOP AT FOUL LINE, MAKE DEFENSE
COMMIT, THEN SHOOT OR FEED UNDER

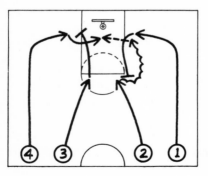

Diagram 7

④ ③ ② ①

Diagram 8

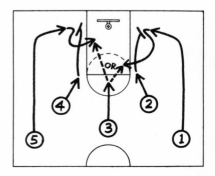

④ ②

⑤ ③ ①

OR

the ball on or near the free-throw line and the other two near the baseline under the goal (Diagram 6). One of the defensive men must commit himself and cover the man with the ball. (If he doesn't, the man at the free-throw line shoots a jump shot.) We fire to whichever of the two baseline men are free, if defense covers the man with the ball.

4. Four-on-three: (Delayed pass out of a rebound.) This is a four-lane pattern. We go in spread out, two men stop at the free-throw line and try to end up with the ball out front, on the foul line. We feel we can do more with the ball on the foul line than on the side. For example, if we can't feed off or get a jump shot, we use moving screens to try and get open.

In Diagram 7, No. 2 ends up with the ball. No. 1 comes back to screen for No. 2 and No. 2 dribbles around screen. No. 3 may then go down and screen for No. 4. No. 4 can come around for the pass from No. 2 under the goal.

5. Five-on-four: (Continuing to push the fast break even though we should have hit already.) Naturally, we try, in this situation, to work the fast break off our normal three lane pattern. This, however, is not always possible (sometimes it is too late). If it is too late, we send in the trailers to each side of the middle man hoping to feed one of them for the driving lay-up or jumper. If the trailers are covered, they can set moving screens for the side men to roll around for jump shots. For example, in Diagram 8, No. 3 has the ball and No. 1 and No. 5 are covered. The trailers, No. 2 and No. 4, are not open, so they go down and set moving screens for No. 1 and No. 5 to roll around for the drive or the jumper.

8.

THE THREE-LANE CONTROLLED FAST BREAK

by Eddie Hickey

Head Basketball Coach (Retired)
Marquette University

*At the end of the 1962–63 season, E. S. Hickey completed
33 years of coaching basketball in a position familiar to him:
At the helm of a successful team playing in a major post-
season tournament (in this case, the NIT where Marquette
finished third). Marquette's appearance in the NIT was the
fourteenth post-season appearance for Eddie Hickey in 25
years of college coaching. His five-year record with the War-
riors is 67–40, and his overall college record is 411–201.*

The three-lane controlled fast break has always been a part of my
offense—at Creighton, St. Louis, and now Marquette. It has with-
stood every rule change. It functions against any type of defense:
multiple, changing, full court, half court, retreat, or any type of
zone. It provides incentive for the smaller player.

With some mastery, it is always a threat and may be turned on or
off at will. You can always "slow down" your attack when once it
has developed but it is neither feasible nor practical to speed up an
attack that has never included the operation of a fast break.

The threat of a fast break worries the opposition, even if you
never use it. The attack against you must be curtailed to prevent
your opportunity "to go." If the opponent penetrates the scoring
area with too many, you can be on your way.

The organization of our controlled three-lane fast break is in three phases. Practice drills to develop these phases are repeated every day.

1. The Scoring Phase: This phase starts at the goal. Players are deployed in groups of three to initiate various kinds of scoring efforts, offensive rebounding, jumping, tipping, area control, passing, receiving, cutting and, occasionally the use of the dribble.

Alignment is shown in Diagram 1. Each player remains identified with his lane until entire lanes are rotated. Each lane has its turn in initiating a scoring effort, starting with the right lane, then the left lane, then the center lane. After this lanes can be rotated.

A scoring effort can start in many ways. Usually, we place the ball on the floor under the goal on the right. The first player on the right line picks up the ball, extends his body, and makes the lay-up shot off the board (unless tall enough to dunk it). If he does not score, the players from the other two lanes converging, in a triangle, on the basket vie for the tip, recovery and shot. All three stay under the basket until the score is made; then a new effort starts with the next man in the right lane. Note these points:

- When all "right" players have initiated an effort, the drill is repeated for the left, then center, lanes.
- Initially, no defense men are used.
- The baseline lanes also work the "angle" sides (Diagram 2), and the center lane players perform without change.

The work proceeds from under the goal, as shown in Diagrams

Diagram 1

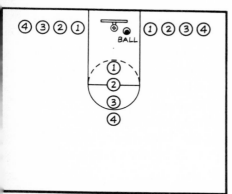

Diagram 2

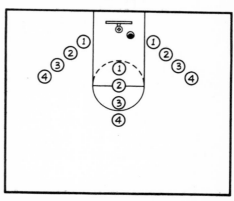

1 and 2, outward, using short, medium, and long-range shots to initiate the effort. Note these two points:

(a) Any type of shot is permitted when the first shot is taken from a distance; most of our players use the jump shot.

(b) As the distance increases, the more the misses; we thus get the work we need on recovery, cutting, passing, jumping, tipping, rebounding, and so on. Remember, the fast break does not always depend on the lay-up shot; this is Utopia.

Initially, no defense is used. As the play is mastered, and distance increases, we add defensive men; first a three-on-one, then a three-on-two, then a three-on-three.

The next step is shown in Diagram 3. The ball is passed between players as all converge on the goal for the scoring effort. Various passing patterns are repeated and the play progresses to the score, after which all players return to their lane line. As practice develops, one, two, or three defensive players are placed near the goal and the development of game condition scrimmage occurs.

When the practice patterns have been developed, player alignment is rotated, and in a short time all players will have the opportunity to develop the skill required for all three lanes.

2. The Initial Phase: This is where the fast break begins. The foundation for the practice patterns is the rebound recovery. The fast break may be developed from other situations such as interceptions, loose-ball recovery, jump ball possession, or "stealing" the ball.

Recovering from out of bounds or after the score offers less opportunities. The rule of stopping the clock and requiring the official to handle the ball on all violations necessarily limits the fast break from out of bounds.

We practice fast break patterns from coverage of the orthodox single pivot attack. Here are four patterns:

Pattern A (Diagram 4): The center rebounds and outlets to the right forward, who "widens" to the side line area (area of least defense). *The "widen" feature is a must in our development.* Patterns then fall in line with the scoring phase (Diagram 3).

Pattern B (Diagram 5): The center rebounds and outlets to the left forward in the middle area, and the "free lance" continuity moves to the scoring phase.

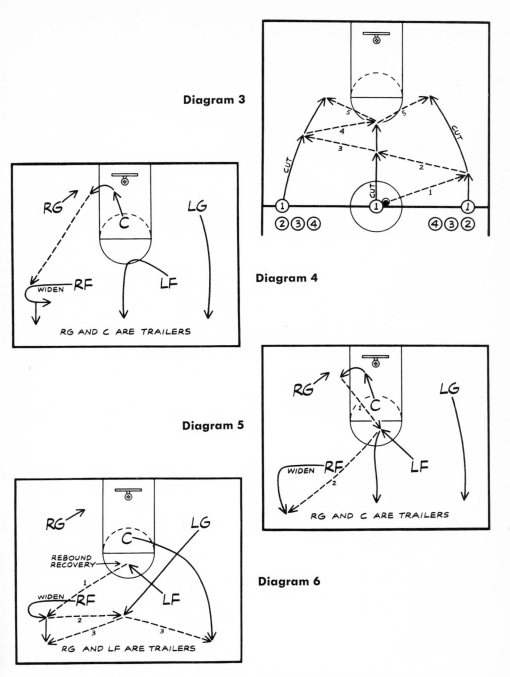

Diagram 3

Diagram 4

Diagram 5

Diagram 6

Pattern C (Diagram 6): The rebound recovery (too deep for the board defense) is made by the out court defensive player, left for-

71

ward. He outlets to the right forward—previously widened to the least defensive area. The "free lance" action follows.

Pattern D (Diagram 7): The rebound recovery is made by the defending weak side base line player, right guard. The outlet pass is made to the widened position occupied by the right forward. Then, except for the outlet, the action repeats Pattern A (Diagram 4).

The defensive coverage is listed as center, forward or guard for purposes of description. The practice patterns function both right and left. In actual play, the outlet possibility sets the play pattern.

When the patterns are understood and developed, one or more players may be added for defensive coverage to simulate game conditions. Eventually, the development progresses to a regular full court "fast break" scrimmage. Excessive dribbling and helter-skelter passing must be avoided. The secret is not in the speed of the players but in the balance of alignment and precision in ball handling and control of the defense.

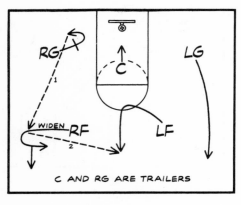

Diagram 7

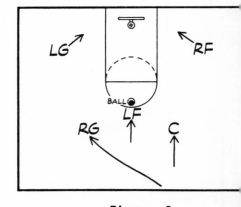

Diagram 8

At the end of the attack, five players are deployed in two distinct "lines." While not required (but advantageous) it is best to have the ball in the possession of the player in the middle lane. Except for trailer options our rule requires the middle player to first "hold up" at the "head of the circle." This is shown in Diagram 8.

3. *The Secondary Phase:* This features options that quickly occur for the trailers previously mentioned. In "trailer" options the middle lane penetrates to the base line and out of the lane. Here he is ready—regardless of size—to function as a single pivot. This penetration often carries the defense clear to the base line and provides options for the trailers to have an immediate scoring opportunity.

9.

MICHIGAN'S SET OFFENSE

by David H. Strack

Head Basketball Coach
University of Michigan

David H. Strack has done one of the great rebuilding jobs in the history of basketball during the five seasons he has coached his Alma Mater, the University of Michigan. From last in the Big Ten with a 2–12 record in 1960–61, to a shared Big Ten title in 1963–64 (with a 23–5 record), and the Big Ten championship in 1964–65 (with a 21–2 record), is enough to qualify the personable Wolverine coach as a "miracle man" by any yardstick.

At the University of Michigan, we believe that team offensive basketball can be divided into three main categories:

1. The teams which place a great emphasis on the fast break— this weapon being the most important offensive function of the team;

2. The teams which control the ball and rarely break and manipulate players—so as to always get the high-percentage shot; and

3. The plan under which we operate—a controlled fast break type of offense, which combines the advantages of the other two and eliminates the disadvantages.

In other words, we will utilize the fast break when the opportunity presents itself, and control the ball for the high-percentage shot when we do not break. Our rule-of-thumb on the fast break is to

try and clear the board quickly and to push the break to its conclusion, which, of course, is the shot—if, and only if, we have a man
advantage; that is, a 3 on 2, or a 2 on 1 situation. We do not want
the shot taken if there is a 3 on 3, 2 on 2, or a 1 on 1 situation.

We do not consider the fast break to be our prime offensive
weapon; it is rather a useful addition to our patterned game.
Whereas defensive basketball is intensity, fierceness, aggressiveness and controlled frenzy—offensive basketball is poise, patience,
precision, definite plans and the ability to meet any situation with
well executed moves. Wishful thinking and "hope" shots only tend
to make any defense look like a "world beater." The good offensive
man is one who moves well *without* the ball and, consequently, a
good offense is one in which all five members are moving. A sound
offense has no place in it for the man who stands still. Keep moving
in a prearranged plan. This keeps the defense moving and will not
allow a defensive man to leave his man and cause trouble elsewhere.
Alertness, of course, is all important in offensive basketball. The
well drilled, poised, offensive player will take the initiative and do
what must be done.

A Set Offense: As a general rule, it's my contention that a shot
may be taken by any player at any time—if it is a shot the boy has
practiced and practiced profusely. It's also a cardinal rule that the
ball should be controlled until such a shot presents itself to a player,
regardless of the time factor. It might come after ten seconds of playing or two minutes. Patience is certainly a virtue in offensive basketball.

A set offense should be geared to accomplish the following:

- Release a boy for a good shot, preferably less than twenty feet.
- When the shot is taken, the floor must be balanced by the
  offense in order to (a) have adequate offensive backboard
  coverage, and (b) have sufficient men in position to guard
  against a fast break.
- A forced shot or pass is something that cannot be tolerated.
When you have the ball, it is not necessary to make this kind of
play. A team skilled in fundamentals and mentally prepared to meet
any and all situations will make a minimum amount of mistakes. No
team can afford the luxury of relinquishing the ball without a shot.

In developing an offense in our practice sessions, we spend a great deal of time on situation basketball. It's the coach's primary duty to prepare his team for any and all situations in which a basketball team might find itself in the course of a season. In building our team offense, we work diligently in preparing offenses to meet any type of defense and function efficiently in any given situation. Our basic offense, however, is one which attacks a man-to-man type defense. The following diagrams illustrate the methods we use in accomplishing this purpose:

GUARD OUTSIDE AND THROUGH SERIES

Basically, we operate from a 2-out 3-in formation, with our post man stationing himself high or low. Our moves in this offense, which we consider disciplined, are keyed on what our guards do; i.e., where do our guards move when they penetrate? Our three basic moves are started when the strong side guard hits the strong side forward and goes outside (swing tight, Diagrams 1, 2, 3 and 4), the guard hits the forward and goes through to the basket (clear, Diagrams 5, 6 and 7), or the guard hits the guard and penetrates to the low post area through the high post (strong, Diagram 8). These moves are triggered by guard moves and are as follows:

Swing Tight—Either Side (Diagrams 1–4): O1 passes to O2 to make defense move. O2 passes to O4 and runs hard to outside corner, being alert for handoff as he passes. O4 pivots with ball toward scoring area. When O5 sees O2 hit O4 and move outside, O5 moves to position approximately 7 feet from basket on weak side of floor. O5 faces ball, O4, and sets screen.

O3 moves across keyhole area to strong side, using O5 as post. O3 must make one way and go the other to confuse defense. O4, with ball, passes to O3 if open and follows pass to cover board. O3 shoots. When O4 passes ball, O2 reverses to take up defensive spot.

If O4 does not hit O3, who has moved across (per Diagram 2), he looks for O5 who, as O3 moves by him, steps to high post situation at foul line and looks for cross court pass. When O4 hits O5, O5 may shoot short jump shot, drive for goal, or hand ball to O1, who drives for goal when cross court pass is thrown.

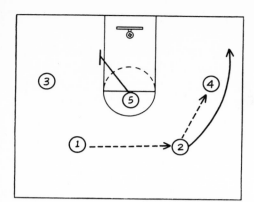

Diagram 1

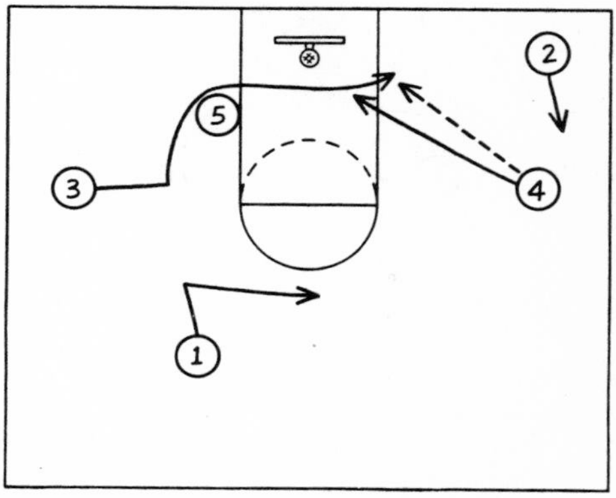

Diagram 2

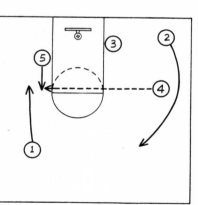

Diagram 3

Diagram 4

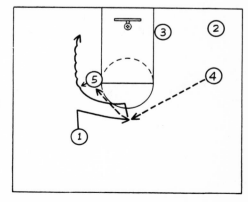

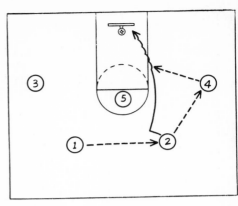

Diagram 5

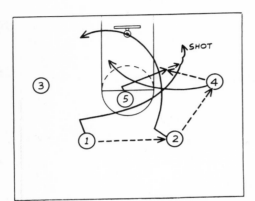

Diagram 6

Diagram 7

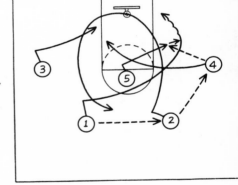

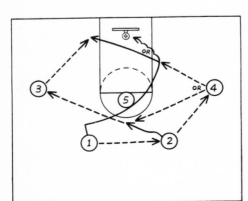

Diagram 8

If O4 does not hit O3, 1st option or O5, 2nd option, he may hit O1, weak side guard, with ball. O1 has faked in and receives ball at position midway between foul lines. O1 then hits O5 at a choke post position and moves off of him in a 2 on 2 basketball move, going outside or down middle trying to get defense to commit an error.

Clear (*Diagrams 5–7:*) O1 passes to O2. O2 passes to O4, steps to inside and moves hard for goal—looking for a return pass from O4. O2's hands are in position to receive pass. If he does, he goes for goal and scores.

As O2 clears toward goal, O5 comes off his tail to a strong side post position. O4 passes to O5 and cuts hard down lane toward basket. O1 fakes left, comes hard off of O4, receives pass from O5 and goes to score.

O2 must move through and to goal and he must move with speed. O2 must clear and circle out as he becomes the safety value defensively.

Strong (*Diagram 8*): O1 hits O2 and O1 moves to low post area going hard off of O5. O2 hits O4 who has two options: First, he may hit O1 as O1 goes to low post. Second, he may reverse ball quickly to O2 who hits O3. We are in a 1–3–1 setup and we remain in it until we shoot.

POST PLAY SERIES

We feel we need a series which features our post man, particularly since we have Bill Buntin, who is a prolific scorer. We call these moves verbally and they are (Red, Diagrams 9 and 10) and (Number, Diagrams 11 and 12).

Red (*Diagrams 9–10*): O1 hits O2, O2 hits O4 and follows. O4 returns ball to O2 and heads for goal. O5 comes off O4's tail and looks for ball. If O5 is high, he fakes toward a weak side low post position and then comes hard off O4's tail. O5 may start low on weak side. O2 hits O5 if possible (this is first and most important option). We want O4 to run a collision course with O5's man.

O3 comes hard to high post and looks for ball. O2 hits O3 as second option. O2 hits O1 as third option, and O1 looks to hit O4 who may have little 10–15 foot jump shot if his man isn't alert. O4, when he gets ball, either shoots or looks for O5 roaming base line.

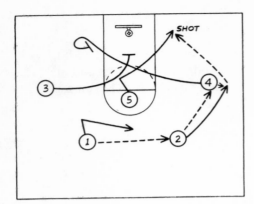

Diagram 9

Diagram 10

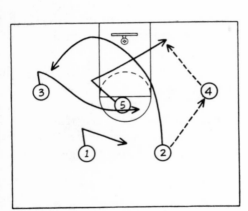

Diagram 11

Diagram 12

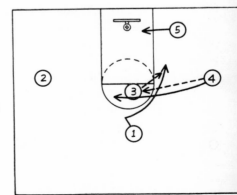

Number (*Diagrams 11–12*): O2 hits O4 and heads for goal. O5, upon hearing number, steps back to weak-side low post and breaks off of O2 as he comes through. O4 hits O5 if possible. O3 heads for high post and looks for ball.

If O4 cannot hit O5, then he looks to hit O3. If O4 hits O3 he follows pass and O1 double cuts off his tail. O1 should be the shooter. O5 has to be alert to move to weak side. If O4 cannot hit either O5 or O3, he reverses to O1 who reverses to O2 and we stay in the 1–3–1, trying to get ball into post man.

This move was put in to utilize the scoring prowess of our center. We found it to be a very effective offensive weapon. We would test any defense at the outset of a game with this maneuver. We know at once, by sending guard through, if defense is man-to-man or zone. The play is cued by our guard calling any number (1–2–3, etc.), or just calling the word "number."

10.

FULL-COURT, COMPETITIVE FAST BREAK DRILLS

by Marion L. Crawley

Head Basketball Coach
Jefferson (Lafayette, Indiana) High School

Marion L. Crawley has been a basketball coach for 33 years, the last 22 at Jefferson High School. His 33-year record is 689–222 and includes 29 sectional (20 in a row), 19 regional, and 4 state championship crowns.

One of the most effective ways to improve the fundamental skills connected with the fast break is through the use of full-court continuous action drills which include teamwork, ball handling, timing and alertness—all learned by the players while moving at top speed.

The use of the full court and the deployment of players on defense in these drills create a teaching situation where the entire squad can get into the action. It is easy for the coach to correct any faulty techniques that show up by stopping the play from time to time to correct mistakes.

The coach should point out time and time again throughout each of these drills that the ball is precious; it must be passed accurately, caught, dribbled, and controlled until a good percentage shot can be made. Wild passes, fumbles, or interceptions must be reduced to a bare minimum if this type of offense is to be of any value. Here are some of the drills that we use and how we work them:

Three Man Pass, Go-Behind Drill (*Diagram 1*): This drill has
the players pass, dribble, and shoot as they move toward the basket
at full speed. It definitely contributes to the development of the fast
break. The drill is a standard one, but we have added some spice. As
the first player arrives at the basket for a lay-up going under either
in a clockwise or counter-clockwise direction, the other two reverse
immediately and circle toward him in the same direction. They each
rebound and pass the ball back until all have taken a lay-up. When
they have, they re-form and start back toward the opposite basket
following the same procedure as above. If the coach feels that the
performance is under par, he can signal repetition until he is satis-
fied.

Five Man Pass and Go-Behind Two (*Diagram 2*): This drill,
too, has been widely used by coaches. However, just as in the preceding drill, we believe we get much greater benefits from it because of the addition of circling, rebounding, and shooting at each

Diagram 1

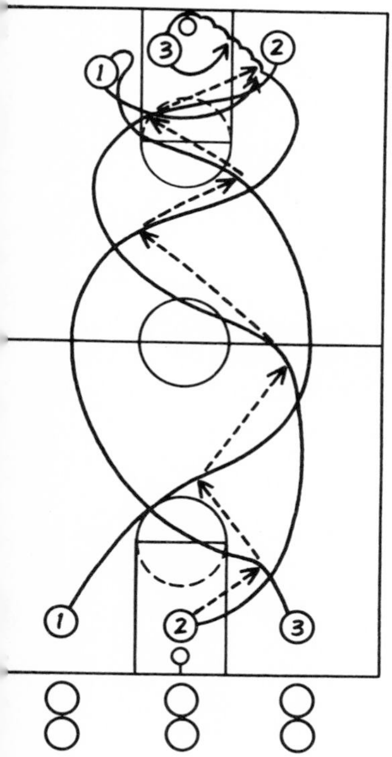

Diagram 2

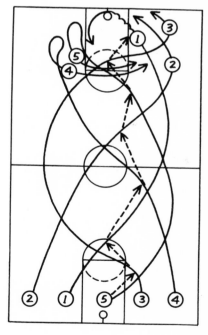

basket by all five players. We also get increased player interest because everybody "gets a word in." The only difference between this and the three man pass, go-behind drill is that five men instead of three are used. Each one passes and goes behind two until arriving at the basket where one takes an under the basket lay-up. When this shot is taken, the other four change and follow in a clockwise or counter-clockwise direction, each rebounding and passing back to the next until all have shot and rebounded.

The drill can teach players better timing if they run in a large circle around the area of the free throw circle. Again, as in the preceding drill, the coach can signal repetitions. Repeating this drill several times takes a great deal of stamina—we have found it to be one of our best conditioners.

Three-on-two, Two-on-one Continuous Action Drill (*Diagram 3*): This is one of our favorite drills and we use it each week throughout the season. It starts by having two lines of players on

Diagram 3   **Diagram 4**

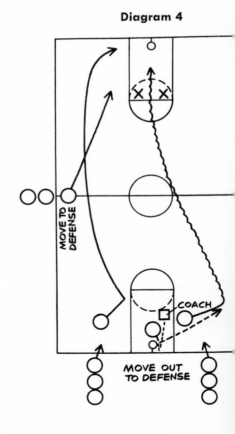

one end of the court ready to take their turns. Two players are placed on defense at the opposite end, either in tandem (most of the time) or in split formation. In the first movement of the drill, we add an extra man in the middle at the offensive end of the court. The coach tosses the ball against the board where it is received by the middle man. The ball is then passed to either side man and the three move down the court to the foul line where the middle man has the option of shooting or passing to the players on either side. The player who started on offense in the left lane then retreats down court with the two original defenders (now on offense) bringing the ball down for the two-on-one situation. This allows the other two original offensive players to remain back as the defense for the next three-on-two maneuver. The drill becomes a continuous three-on-two, two-on-one with the entire squad working the action. The key to the whole thing is to watch the action of player A. He first starts in the left lane, then retreats by himself on defense against the two original defensive men, picks up these two men and advances up the court on offense, remains there with a partner on defense until they get possession of the ball for a two man drive to the basket where they both retire to the ends of the lines.

To give players practice in advancing the ball against pressure, we bring the two defensive men up to the front court, where they try to stop the break before it crosses the 10-second line. After this they retreat close to the basket and take their turn there on defense. This pressure defense causes the offense to adjust and to make different moves to be able to work the ball up the floor.

Three-on-two Continuous Action Drill (Diagram 4): This drill is started by the coach throwing the ball up against the board with three players waiting to rebound and break. It is designed to provide a continuous three-on-two situation. A third defensive man works into the play after the three players breaking down the floor have passed the mid-line. He moves in late to help on defense if the two initial defensive players can stall the break temporarily for him to get in position.

When the ball is recovered by one of the players on defense, he starts a fast break pattern toward the opposite basket along with the other two men. The three players just completing the fast break move off the floor, and one joins the line at mid-court, while the

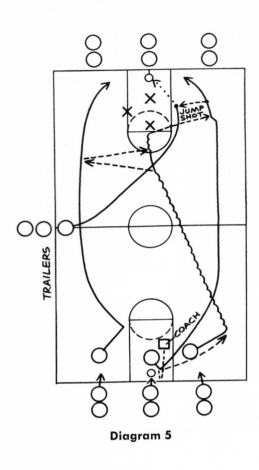

Diagram 5

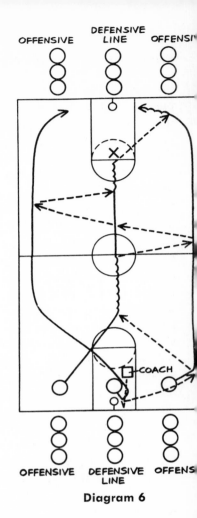

Diagram 6

two remaining ones go to the ends of the lines off the floor under the basket.

The two defensive men may use the tandem formation—one behind the other—or a split defense. This gives the players working against them excellent practice in reacting to the various tactics of the defense.

Three-on-three Continuous Action with a Trailer (Diagram 5): This drill brings into play a fourth man as a trailer. Three lines of players are stationed at each end of the court and one line at midcourt. As in the previous drill, the coach starts the action by throwing the ball up against the board with three defensive players at the opposite basket. When the three breaking men pass midcourt, the fourth player comes on from the side as a trailer. He breaks to either side of the middle man looking for a pass. If he gets the ball, he may shoot from near the foul line or drive on into the basket for a lay-up. When the middle man is stopped, he may pass to either side man, then cut on through to clear the floor for the trailer. When the defense recovers the ball, they break for the opposite basket where they will be opposed by three players who have come from the lines under the basket. When players have completed their turn, three join the lines at the end and one goes to the line along the side of the court.

Competitive Continuous Action Three-on-one Drill (*Diagram 6*): When a three-on-one fast break situation comes up, the numerical advantage should provide a good lay-up shot. We work on this in this drill. Three lines of players are formed at each end of the floor. Those in the middle line become defensive men while those in the two outside lines become offensive men making it possible to keep a continuous three-on-one situation going at all times. Again, the coach throws the ball against the board to start the drill. The middle man rebounds and tosses to one of the side men cutting toward the sideline. The ball is passed or dribbled to a player in the middle area where it is advanced by passing not more than once to either side man and back to the middle man who dribbles to the defensive man. He then fakes with his head and eyes and makes a low bounce pass to either side man for a lay-up shot. To correctly execute this key pass, the player should bend well forward at the waist to be in a position to make a low bounce pass under the arms of the defensive man. At the conclusion of each break, the defensive man recovers the ball and passes out to one of the two players who have just come from the outside lines to a position on the floor ready to go the moment the ball is captured by the defensive man. The two offensive men who just completed play move to ends of lines to await their turn again. The defensive position is filled each time by a player from the middle line who should move up near the center of the floor ready to retreat when opposed by three men breaking toward the goal he is defending.

11.

OFFENSIVE SERIES
OFF THE BASIC SHUFFLE

by James A. Kinion

Head Basketball Coach
John A. Holmes (Edenton, N.C.) High School

Coaching in a small rural school (150 enrollment) Jim Kinion built up a 10-year record of 157–24 at Pantego (North Carolina) High School. In this time, he won five county championships, two district championships, and participated twice in the state tournament. At present, James Kinion is head basketball coach at John A. Holmes High School.

In addition to being an ideal offense for the team with no big man, I feel the shuffle encourages teamwork and builds confidence. In our version we use the standard Drake shuffle with two additional play series.

In discussing our attack, I prefer to name the positions rather than number them (Diagram 1). To make the offense more effective, I feel the man who brings the ball down court should work into the cutter position. With the ball in this position, we can go into our first, second, or third series.

First Series: Ball goes from cutter to point man to feeder. If the defense overplays the point man, the point man and feeder interchange. The feeder sets up at the low post position (Diagram 1) and must fake to break out and receive the pass. Then the cutter breaks off the center in as close a cut as possible. If the cutter does

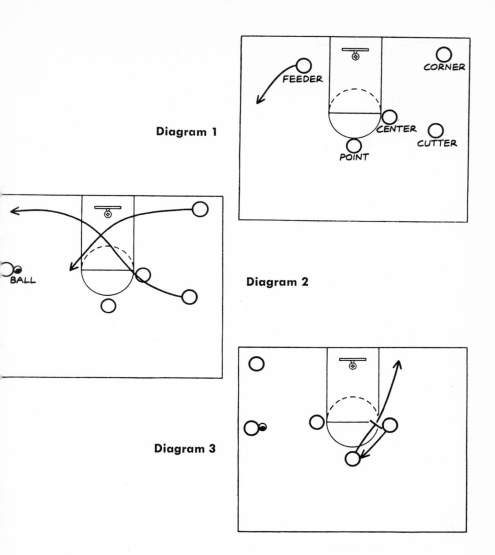

Diagram 1

FEEDER

CORNER

CENTER

CUTTER

POINT

Diagram 2

BALL

Diagram 3

not receive the pass, he goes through to the corner. As the cutter starts his move, the corner man comes along the baseline and cuts into the free throw lane area on the opposite side from the present center (Diagram 2). The point man moves to his right and sets a screen for the center who moves out to the point position. The point man continues through to the low post position (Diagram 3).

Player interchange is as follows: (a) Cutter to corner; (b) corner to center; (c) center to point; (d) point to feeder; (e) feeder to cutter. The ball goes to the point man and the series is run to the opposite side (Diagram 4).

89

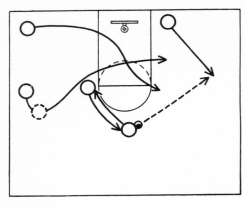

Diagram 4

Diagram 5

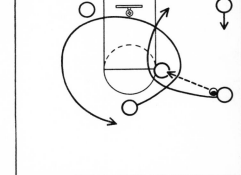

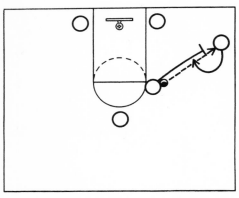

Diagram 6

Second Series: Ball is in cutter position. Cutter bounces to center, and cutter and point man run a scissors off the center (Diagram 5). If the center can't work a shot, he passes to the corner man and sets up a screen for him. The corner man drives off the screen for a shot or gives back to the center if there is a switch on defense (Diagram 6).

The two men under the boards rebound and the corner man, if he shoots, crashes along the boards along with the center for the rebound, leaving one man out for defense. We alternate three and four men on the boards, depending on the game situation and the team we are playing.

90

Third Series: This begins with the cutter passing to the corner and going through, watching for a pass back from the corner, if the defensive man lags. As soon as the pass is made to the corner, the center rolls and sets a screen for the feeder; it should be set outside the three-second area and the feeder breaks for a shot if possible (Diagram 7). The feeder comes across the lane and then goes back and sets up at the free throw lane on the opposite side. The players should then be in the position shown in Diagram 8.

The corner man dribbles out toward the point man who comes to meet him and receives the ball. The corner man goes to the point position. The man who started the series as cutter cuts off

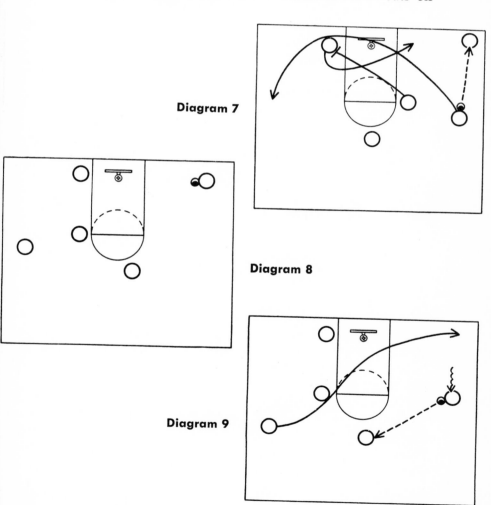

Diagram 7

Diagram 8

Diagram 9

center and receives a pass from the point man if possible (Diagram 9). If no shot is set up, the cutter goes to the corner, the center changes positions to the opposite side, and the team is ready to run either of the three series.

SWITCHING DEFENSES

The three patterns discussed are used against teams that do not switch on defense; naturally most teams switch in some instances. Our offense ran into difficulties against a team with a big man when the big man sagged off the center and jammed our offense. The two switches that gave us trouble were the switch by the defensive center on the cutter in the first series, and the switch on the low post man in our third series.

We use the following movements to combat the switches:

In the *first* series, when the center was switching, the cutter went through and stopped at the low post position. The center then re-

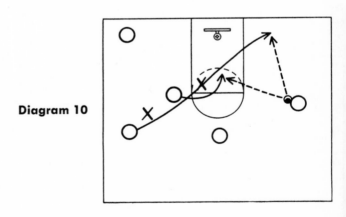

Diagram 10

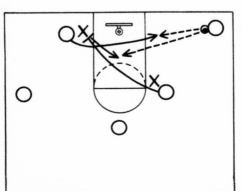

Diagram 11

versed and came to the free throw lane area for a quick pass from the feeder for a jump shot. If the defensive center does not follow up the switch, then the feeder hits the cutter for a quick jump shot, or a possible feed to the center if he has good shooting position on the defensive man (Diagram 10). I like to have the opponent's big man guarding our feeder. If he does not come out and takes the center, this movement will bring him out.

If our best shooter is in the cutter position, the center who has switched must come out and guard the cutter, thereby giving us more driving room on our next series. The tip-off to our players on the switch must be picked up by the man setting the screen; he glances over his shoulder and if the switch is taking place, he makes his move as shown in Diagram 10.

In our *third* series, we use a similar move to combat the switch on the low post man. If there is a switch on the man coming across, the man who sets the screen breaks quickly into the three-second area for a quick pass and possible shot (Diagram 11).

12.

SHUFFLE PATTERNS FOR TIGHT DEFENSES

by ROBERT BENNETT

Head Basketball Coach
Lompoc (California) High School

Robert Bennett has been head basketball coach at Lompoc High School since 1956. During that time, he has turned out 2 league championship teams, 2 runners-up, 2 CIF AA play-off teams and 2 state tournament teams. His over-all basketball record is 188 wins against 98 losses.

At Lompoc High School, we always attempt to fast break against any type defense—but if we can't score, we set up and run our shuffle patterns. Against man-to-man and tight defenses, we use what we call the Shuffle #1 and Shuffle #2. It's been a winning offense for us. If run right, the shuffle will give you continual movement of all players. It's a continuity pattern and does not work if any player loafs or does not run the pattern. You've got to hustle. Here's how it works:

SHUFFLE #1

Diagram 1 shows the basic position of players at the beginning of the pattern. Center is always on opposite side of the ball. Guard with ball will penetrate as far as defense will allow. Forwards line up with free-throw line.

Diagram 2: After guard is stopped on his drive, he will pass to the forward on the side line. It is up to the forward to fake in and come out to meet the pass. Guard #1 drives to saddle. Center #5 fakes in and goes to saddle. #1 and #5 form a double screen. Guard #2 must take his defensive man to the outside then run him into double screen as he drives around #1 and #5 down center. If #2 is open, #3 will pass to him. If #2 is not open, he will go to the corner. #4 will fake in then out at same time this is going on.

Diagram 3: #4 will break to center then down and around double screen. If #4 is open, he receives pass from #3. If he is not open, he will go to the free-throw lane.

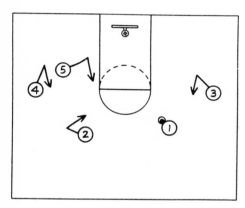

Diagram 1

Diagram 2

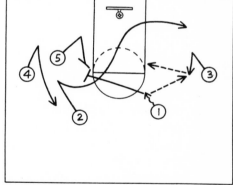

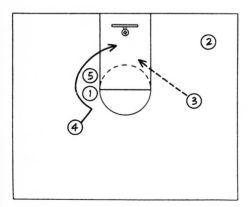

Diagram 3

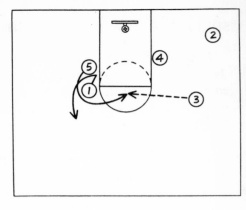

Diagram 4

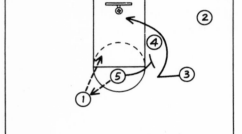

Diagram 5

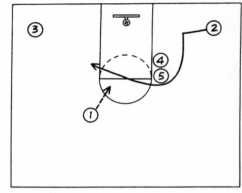

Diagram 6

Diagram 4: If first two options fail to produce, continue on with pattern. #1 fakes in; #5 uses fake as screen and goes to free-throw line where he will receive pass from #3. If open, he drives. If he is not open, he passes out to #1.

Diagram 5: After #5 passes off, he goes to saddle to form double screen with #4. #3 drives toward free throw line, then behind double screen. If #3 is open, he will receive pass from #1. If he is not open, he goes to the opposite corner.

Diagram 6: #2 drives around double screen. #1 will pass to him if he is open. If not open, #2 will go to the saddle.

Diagram 7: #5 fakes in and goes to the outside. #4 uses #5's fake as a screen and drives to free-throw line and receives the pass

96

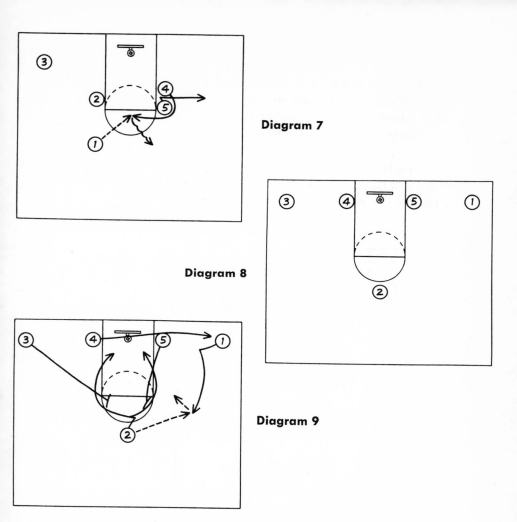

Diagram 7

Diagram 8

Diagram 9

from #1. If open, he shoots. If not open, he dribbles out. You have completed the continuity pattern, and you start again.

SHUFFLE #2

Player Position: Diagram 8 shows the basic set up of this pattern. We use it only against tight defenses.

Diagram 9: #2 passes to #1 who has faked in and come out to meet the pass. #5 and #3 go to the free-throw line to set up screens. #4 goes to #1 position. #2 has option to drive around either #3 or #5.

Diagram 10: #2 will receive pass from #1 if open. If not open, he will clear out of lane and return back to original position. #1 will pass to #4 if #2 is not open.

Diagram 11: #5 screens for #3 who drives to solid divider on free-throw lane. He will receive pass from #4 or #1 if he is open.

Diagram 12: #3 will clear out if he does not receive the pass. #5 will roll down right side of the lane after setting screen. He will receive pass if open.

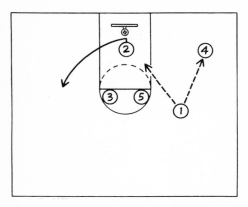

Diagram 10

Diagram 11

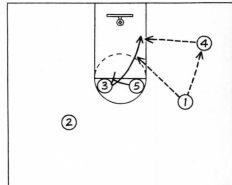

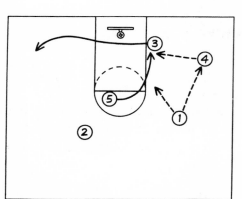

Diagram 12

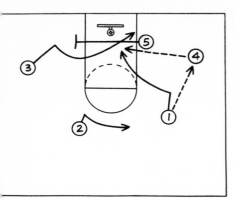

Diagram 13

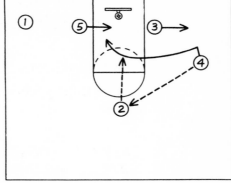

Diagram 14

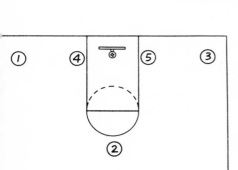

Diagram 15

Diagram 13: #5 will screen for #3 who drives across free throw lane. #1 drives down the center; if open he will receive the pass.

Diagram 14: #4 passes out to #2 and drives to lane. If open, he receives pass; if not open, he goes to free-throw lane. #5 and #3 move to positions.

Diagram 15: You are now set up to start pattern again.

13.

OPTIONS FOR THE SHUFFLE OFFENSE

by HAROLD COLE

Head Basketball Coach
Knox Central (Barbourville, Kentucky) High School

Harold Cole's five-year record as head basketball coach at Knox Central High School is 111 wins against 28 losses. During that time, his squads have two conference championships and three district championships.

We have always been a strong contender for the Conference championship—but only after the adoption of the shuffle as our basic offense were we able to bring home the "hardware." We decided to make this radical change in our offensive pattern for the following reasons:

1. Foremost in our minds was the fact that to play this offense properly requires a real team effort. We have never been blessed with the super star around which we could build an offense. But to say this offense stifled individual play would be an injustice; all of our graduating front line of last season received full athletic grants to colleges.

2. We also felt that the shuffle capitalized on two shots that boys like to perform—the driving layup and the jump shot from 15 to 18 feet. If you will notice boys when they "choose up" and play half court, these two shots will dominate the game. The basic prin-

ciple of the shuffle is to drive for the basket for the layup, and if this fails, have a jump shooter in the vacuum created by the drive.

3. Then, too, we liked the idea of the challenge presented to us and the boys in learning the shuffle—as it requires each boy to learn all positions. The boys responded well to the challenge of "something new" and really bore down on the homework.

The shuffle will demand a great deal of your time in learning how to coach it. Just as it is with any offense, attention to the little things is what makes it go. Also, you must adjust this offense to your personnel; don't "copy" the shuffle as prescribed by anyone—but read all you can on the various systems and adjust them to your particular situation.

The following are some of the moves that have worked well for us at Knox Central High School:

• *Floor Positions:* The floor positions are numbered to simplify it for player digestion—and for coach and player communication. The overload may be set up on either side of the floor according to player strength and ball handling ability. Diagram 1 shows the overload left and the numbers used for player positions.

• *First Option:* The first option is a simple cross with #5 screen-

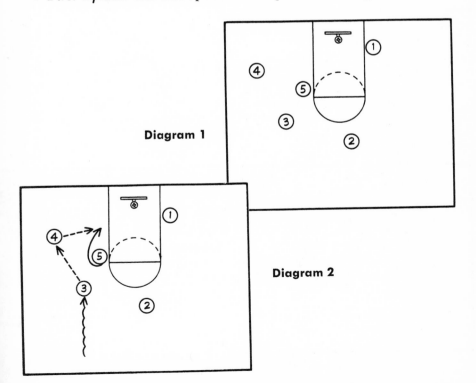

Diagram 1

Diagram 2

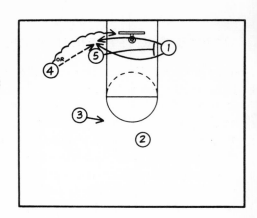

Diagram 3

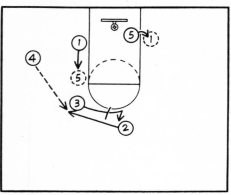

Diagram 4

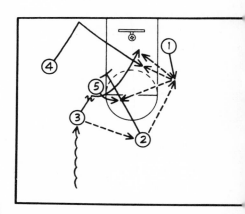

Diagram 5

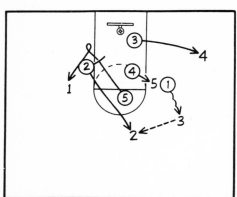

Diagram 6

ing for #1. The 5 man may be free here on his first move as he does a reverse pivot (Diagram 2) and looks for a pass from #4.

• *Second Option:* If he doesn't break free, he crosses the lane to screen for #1 who takes the base line cut as in Diagram 3. #4 may also beat his man on the base line. Providing a shot is not taken from either of these, #1 and #5 exchange spots and #3 and #2 change (Diagram 4). We are now ready to run another option.

• *Third Option:* This is the basic pattern of the shuffle. The individual assets for the different positions and our keys for the different options will not be included. Adjustments to the pattern and rotations of the continuity of players are changed each year to fit the personnel available.

The 2 or 3 man may bring the ball up the floor. The option starts with a pass from the 2 to the 1 man. The 3 man sets his man up for the screen by shuffling his feet and feinting to one side of the 5 man, who positions himself for #3 to hang his man on. He then makes his cut to the basket to either side of #5 as in Diagram 5.

The 1 man hits 3 if he is free, beats his man for a layup, or a 12 to 15 foot jump shot. If he has failed to get the good shot, he is looking for #4, who started his move at the same time as #3. He cuts directly at the base line four feet from the foul lane. He then plants his left foot and cuts at the #1 man moving right off #3's cut. The 1 man is also looking for #5 who is rolling over the top of #2's screen for a 15 foot jump shot.

• *The Rotation:* The rotation must be done quickly to be effective. Diagram 6 shows the new positions when the option fails to produce the desirable percentage shot. The 1 man with the ball backs out to the 3 spot. We run #5 inside #2, screening for him and exchanging spots to become the new feeder or #1 man. The 2 man moves away from the basket back to the 2 spot to become the point man and play maker. #4 moves in the 5 spot and 3 goes to 4.

• *Fourth Option:* The fourth option starts the same as the third with #3 cutting off #5. Many teams will sag the 4 defensive man to help stop the 3 cut. When this happens, we double screen at the foul lane for #4 rolling over the top for the 12 foot jump shot (Diagram 7). The 5 man screens with his back to #4 so that he may roll under the basket for the high pass from #1 or #4.

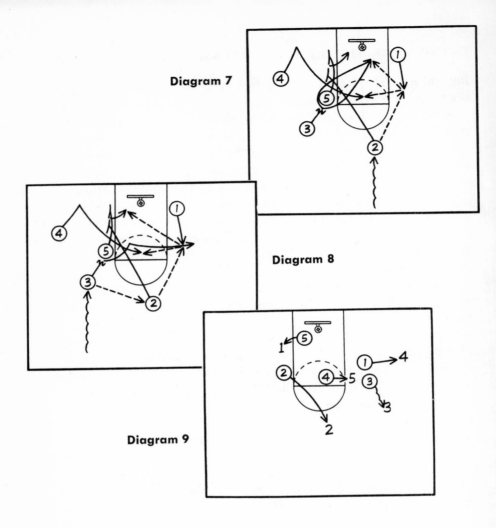

Diagram 7

Diagram 8

Diagram 9

Several teams will switch their 5 defensive man to 3. When this happens, the 3 man may make a jump shot. Usually the defensive pivot man will not follow #3 away from the basket which makes this even more effective. He is also looking for #4 coming over the double screen (Diagram 8).

• *The Rotation:* The rotation of the fourth option is the same as the third. Diagram 9 shows the rotation when #3 cuts over the top of #1. If #4 is a fair ball handler, he may be allowed to rotate to the 2 spot with #5 returning to the same position and #3 rolling out to #3. The rotation can be adjusted to best serve the team.

• *Circle Movement:* The defense will usually be set to defend against your bread and butter options from specific positions. There

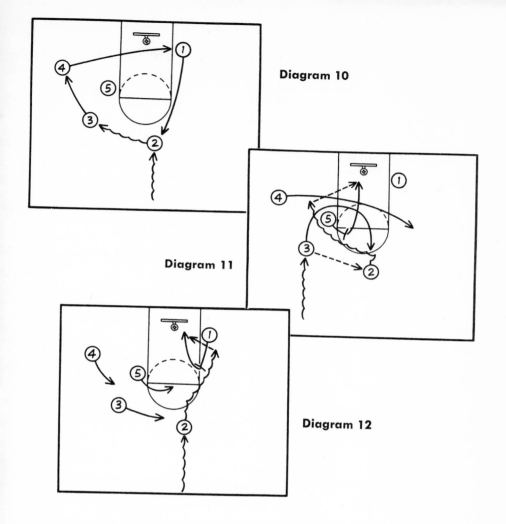

Diagram 10

Diagram 11

Diagram 12

are several variations used to help keep them from overplaying your best boys and floating the other defenders to help out on them. Diagram 10 illustrates one of the circle moves we use to maneuver the defensive personnel into any defensive area we want them. This forces them to play in a more or less unfamiliar place. It may be used one or more times in succession to accomplish the desired positions; it is also effective against combination defenses. Circle left movement is illustrated here—we also employ the circle right.

• *Clearout:* This is effective when the defense is overshifting to your weak side. It is a fine strong side maneuver and tends to keep them squared off man-for-man. The 2 man has the ball, #3 and #4 clear the overloaded side by cutting across the lane, as in Diagram

11. The #5 man then moves to his left to screen for #2 who feints to the right to set his man up for #5 to position. He may drive off #5 to go all the way or give to #5 who has rolled under the basket after a switch has been executed. A 15-foot jump shot also may be evident if the switch is followed up.

• *Back Block and Roll:* Due to the overload, the weak side is clear for a pick and roll by #1 and #2 as in Diagram 12. The #2 man will go all the way, jump shoot or if a good switch is made, he will pass to #1 rolling under the basket. This is most effective when your #2 man is being played very aggressively.

14.

A "REVOLVING-CUTTER" ZONE OFFENSE

by BILL QUENETTE

Head Basketball Coach
Peninsula (Port Angeles, Washington) College

Bill Quenette's first 4 years as a basketball coach were spent as an assistant at Concordia (Minnesota) College where his teams compiled a 46–12 record. When Peninsula College opened, he took over as head basketball coach and his teams are now giving the older, more established teams in the league something to worry about.

I used to be an advocate of the stationary 1-3-1 basketball offense against the 2-3 or 2-1-2 zone defense. Seeing a team, however, play a variation of this offense where they kept the middle open to allow a player to break in caused me to experiment with better ways of operating the zone offense. My feeling now is that if you station a man in the middle of the zone and have him stay there throughout the offensive pattern, you are, in effect, playing your offense with four men. The defense is alert to his being in the middle and can cover him better because they know where he will be at all times. By placing him elsewhere and leaving the middle open, you can break a player in from anywhere on the court—this gives your offense the element of surprise which is so essential to success.

ODD OR EVEN

I now like to consider zone defenses as being either "odd" or "even" in much the same way a football coach considers different defensive line sets. The "even" zone defenses are those that have an even number of men up front and the "odd" zones are those which have an odd number of men in the defensive guard position. We have a definite offense alignment for each of these types.

Offensing the "Even" Zone Defenses: Against a 2-3 or 2-1-2 ("even") zone defense, which seems to be the most common in to-day's basketball, we line up in a 1-2-2 as shown in Diagram 1. No. 2 and No. 3 line up high on an extension of the free throw line, and in as close as the defense will allow them to get a shot off. These two men are very important to the offense and must be able to shoot well from 20 feet out. No. 4 and No. 5 are just outside the free throw lane off the baseline. They must not position themselves behind the backboard because many times they can get a direct pass from the quarterback (No. 1) and must be in position to shoot immediately. We put our biggest men here because it gives us better offensive rebound strength (the second and third shots are very important to our zone offense).

If the defensive men X-4 and X-5 concern themselves with preventing our two wingmen (No. 2 and No. 3) from shooting and playing too high, it is fairly easy for No. 1 to pass directly into either No. 4 or No. 5 for an easy shot attempt. If X-4 and X-5 back in to provide better coverage of the two baseline men, No. 2 and No. 3 will have all the time they need to get off a good shot from the side. This offensive alignment puts real pressure on the two deep men in the zone defense. If the center (X-1) backs up to support the baseline, we allow either No. 4 and No. 5 or No. 2 and No. 3 to break into this large middle area for a pass and possible shot (Diagram 2).

By bringing one of the baseline men up, we can position ourselves in the traditional 1-3-1 attack still used by many coaches. We can operate from this set up or return back to our original positions if a pass and shot does not develop.

Our revolving-cutter offense starts when the ball is passed to one

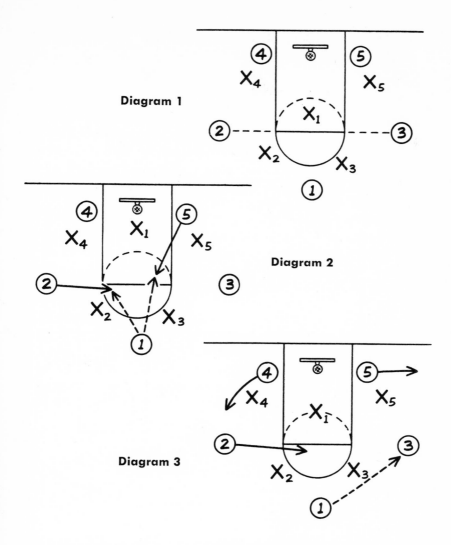

Diagram 1

Diagram 2

Diagram 3

of the wingmen and we have the offensive alignment break as in Diagram 3.

As the pass is made to No. 3, No. 5 moves out towards the corner no further than 15 to 20 feet from the basket. It helps if the two baseline players can shoot from this position because they will have many opportunities against zone defenses. As the ball goes to No. 3, No. 2 also initiates his break into the vacant center area. As shown in Diagram 3, No. 4 starts toward the spot vacated by No. 2. We do this to make it possible to have a player immediately available for a shot attempt from the weakside should the

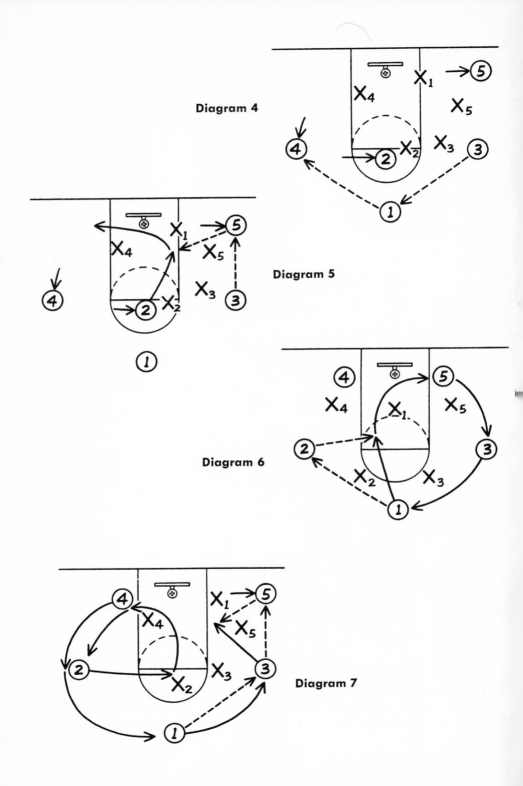

Diagram 4

Diagram 5

Diagram 6

Diagram 7

defense overshift too far. The pass would go immediately back to No. 1 and then over to No. 4 for the easy jump shot (Diagram 4).

Diagram 5 shows how the cuts are made when the ball goes from wingman No. 3 to baseline man No. 5. No. 2, who had broken to the free throw line with the pass to No. 3, now breaks down toward the basket looking for a pass from No. 5. This is especially effective if defense covers the corner man (No. 5) with X-1 as is often the case. If No. 2 does not receive a pass, he continues on and sets up in the spot vacated by No. 4. We can now start all over again with a player in each of the original starting positions. All that has been done is to rotate or revolve two players on the weakside (side away from the ball). The play gives us an excellent threat in the middle to keep the defense honest and also gives us a chance to work the ball back to the weakside for a good shot. Breaking No. 2 into the middle will usually cause the defense to forget about the possibility of our having someone stationed on the weakside. No. 4 can break up to this position unnoticed. When the ball goes down the left side of the court, the same breaks are executed by No. 3 and No. 5 on the weakside. Our boys enjoy the chance to play several positions in this offense and have an opportunity to shoot and score from both inside and outside.

We have these two rules in running this offensive arrangement: (1) the wingman on the weakside must always cut into the middle towards the ball as it is played down the side; and (2) when a player vacates his position to make a break down the middle for the ball, the player next to him must fill his spot (fill towards the ball). For example in Diagram 6, if the ball was passed from No. 1 to No. 2 on the left side and No. 1 decided to break into the middle for a pass and a shot, it would be No. 3's responsibility to fill his vacated spot while No. 5 filled for No. 3. With this rule, we could have any of the five offensive players break or cut into the middle if the area provided an opportunity for a possible shot.

We do use one other variation of this "even" offensive alignment. In Diagram 7, No. 2 has made his cut from the free throw line towards the basket (perhaps prematurely) and did not receive the pass so he continued on to fill the baseline spot. No. 3, noticing an opening in the middle of the defense, makes a cut toward the basket to receive a pass from No. 5 for the shot. No. 1 then fills for

No. 3, No. 4 for No. 1, and No. 2 ends up back in his original position with No. 3 filling the vacated baseline position if he didn't receive the ball. This gives us two cuts in the middle and we still have a player occupying each of the original floor positions.

This maneuver does not leave us in the best rebound position because we have the big man out front and the small one under the basket. When we continue the continuity, however, we usually get a shot sometime during the exchange and we do not have to have our big man too far from the basket for too long.

Offensing the "Odd" Zone Defenses: Against the 1-2-2 or 1-3-1 ("odd") zone defense, we use the same theory of attack as we do

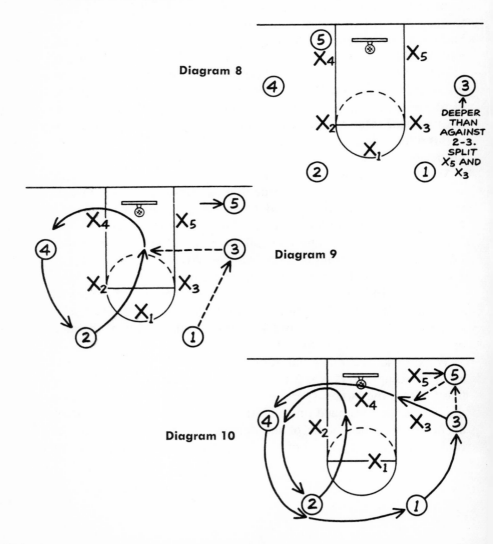

Diagram 8

Diagram 9

Diagram 10

against "evens" but begin from different starting position. If we were to continue in the 1-2-2, the 1-2-2 zone defense could play us practically man-for-man and still be in a zone. Diagram 8 shows our basic "odd" alignment. We attack both the 1-2-2 and the 1-3-1 zones the same way. No. 5 tries to position himself on the ball side of the baseline and roams from corner to corner. When either of the two front men (No. 1 or No. 2) have the ball, we allow any of the remaining three to make a break to the middle of the zone for a pass and shot.

However, when the ball goes to one of the wingmen as in Diagram 9, we want the other front man (No. 2 in the diagram) to break down the middle for a pass. As No. 2 vacates his position, No. 4 fills for him to be ready for a pass back to the weakside and a shot. No. 5 moves out towards the corner as No. 3 receives the ball from No. 1. This weakside rotating cut can continue by No. 2 and No. 4 as long as the ball is on the right side of the floor. Again, as No. 3 makes the pass to No. 5 at the baseline, he can cut to the basket for a return pass from No. 5 (Diagram 10). If he does this, No. 1 must fill for him. No. 4 would then fill for No. 1 and No. 2 would come back to his original spot.

Ball Side Overload: Breaking No. 2 into the middle against the "odd" zone defenses provides a very definite ball side overload which, in essence, is the strategy used by many coaches against the zone defense.

15.

AN OFFENSIVE TECHNIQUE AGAINST THE ZONE

by CAL LUTHER

Head Basketball Coach
Murray (Kentucky) State College

Cal Luther completed his 6th straight winning season in (1964–65) as head basketball coach at Murray State College with a 19–7 record. He was voted "Coach of the Year" in the Ohio Valley Conference during the 1963–64 season when he captured his school's first conference title. Before coming to Murray State, Coach Luther gained similar honors in a four-year tenure at DePauw University.

Every modern day basketball team, high school or college, must have an offensive attack capable of combating the ever present zone defense. Playing against zone defenses today requires an offensive technique which can exploit most of the weak spots of the standard zone defenses, and which is versatile enough to adjust to the many zone variations.

Several ingredients are necessary in your offensive pattern: 1) Player movement as well as ball movement is imperative. 2) You must penetrate to the weak spots of the zone for the good percentage shot. 3) It must provide the opportunity to get the second shot at the goal, the rebound shot. 4) The attack should offer adequate defensive balance.

At Murray State College we use a variable zone attack that contains all the necessary ingredients. Here's the way it works:

• *Zone Defense Similarities:* Most of the standard zone defenses—2-1-2, 2-3, 3-2, 1-3-1, 1-2-2—cover the ball in approximately the same manner once it reaches the baseline area (Diagrams 1 & 2). For this reason, the interior attack against most zone defenses can be relatively the same. Our interior attack attempts to take advantage of these zone defensive similarities.

• *Initial Phase of Our Attack:* Diagram 3 shows the initial phase of our attack. Starting from a 1-3-1 alignment, the point man (1) passes to the wing man on the right (2), who in turn

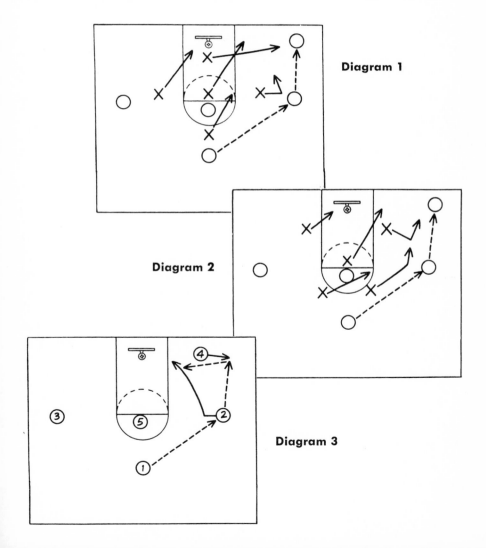

Diagram 1

Diagram 2

Diagram 3

hits the baseline man (4), who moves out quickly from a tight position to meet the pass. The wing man (2), as soon as he makes his pass to the baseline man (4), immediately takes a sharp cut for the goal looking for the return pass from the baseline man. If the wing man is being aggressively defensed, he must first make his initial fake step to his left or right in order to prevent the defensive from "jamming him up" and preventing his quick movement through the zone. This move is particularly effective against those zoned defenses which play only a single man on the back line of the defense, such as the 1-3-1.

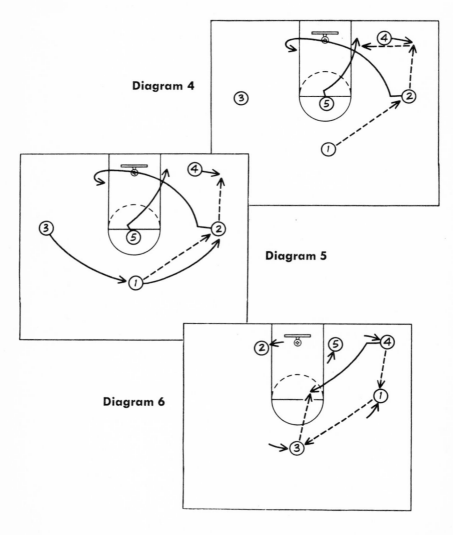

Diagram 4

Diagram 5

Diagram 6

• *Diagram 4:* In Diagram 4, you will note that as soon as the wing man (2) begins his quick cut through the defense, the high post man (5) makes his move toward the post area and times his cut so that the instant the 2 man clears the low post area and fails to receive the return pass, he hooks into the area in front of the defensive man assigned to that zone. If he breaks into this area sharply and he is open, he will immediately receive the pass from the baseline man (4). We have found this to be an excellent option particularly when our high post man is a scoring threat and has some cleverness at handling the ball inside the defense. It also gives us excellent rebounding position with our wing man (2) on the weak side of the board.

• *Diagram 5:* If the baseline man (4) is able to pass into the post man (5), he immediately swings to the inside of the defense to cover the middle on the offensive board. As soon as the wing man (2) makes his "quick cut" through the defense, his position is immediately taken by the point man (1) and the point is immediately filled by the opposite wing man (3).

• *Diagram 6:* If the baseline man (4) is unable to take advantage of either of the first two options, he then immediately return passes to the wing man who quickly passes to the point position. The baseline man then cuts into the middle of the defense "wherever the daylight is" timing the cut, with the ball reaching the point position.

The timing here is extremely important for against a normal zone defense, the cuts of the wing man (2) and the high post man (5) will cause the interior of the zone to sink and defense the baseline area. Then as the ball quickly moves around the perimeter of the zone, and the zone begins to react back out to cover the ball in its movement, the interior of the zone will open up. If the baseline man (4) times his cut well and the point man (3) is capable of making the pass, this is an extremely effective maneuver giving the good inside shot to the baseline man (5) and the wing man (2).

• *Diagram 7:* Diagram 7 follows the continuity to the weak side of the floor. If the point man (3) is unable to make the pass inside the defense to the baseline man (4), he then quickly passes to the wing man (2) who breaks up from the baseline on the weak side of the floor. He should break up into position to receive the pass so that he is facing the goal at a 45° angle ready to shoot the "short jumper" the instant he receives the pass if he is not covered.

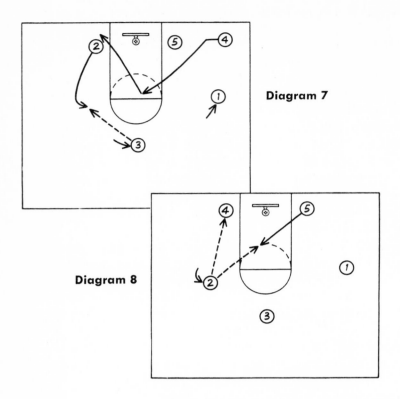

Diagram 7

Diagram 8

• *Diagram 8:* If the baseline man (4) does not receive the pass, the instant he makes his quick cut into the middle of the defense, then he immediately cuts sharply to the weakside baseline area. When the wing man (2) receives the pass on the weak side, if the timing is good, he should have 3 basic options:

1. First of all, the good jump shot, if not covered;

2. Secondly, if he is covered, the opportunity to make the quick pass to the baseline man (4) breaking to the weakside baseline area;

3. Thirdly, if he is covered and the baseline man is likewise covered, he should have the opportunity to pass inside the defense to the post man (5) hooking his man inside the lane.

Should none of these 3 options materialize because of spacing or timing or defensive adjustment, then the offensive continuity is ready to begin from the weak side of the floor with the baseline man (4) stepping out and the 2 man making his pass to him and starting his initial cut through the defense once more.

118

I have found this to be a very effective basic offensive technique against the zone defense. Naturally, it is necessary to add some variations and counter-moves to be used against what I call "screw-ball" and "match-up" zone defenses. However, we have found that these can readily be worked into our basic offensive pattern against the zone.

16.

PRESSURE OFFENSE

by FORDDY ANDERSON

Head Basketball Coach
Michigan State University

An eighteen year coaching veteran with a 314–180 record, Forrest "Forddy" Anderson is one of the most respected names in the profession. Coming to Michigan State after a 142–55 record at Bradley, he made the Spartans a name to contend with in the Big Ten. He coached the first Michigan State team to compete in an NCAA play-off, and a team that won more games (19) than any other in State history.

Today, a lot of emphasis is being placed on pressure defense. We suggest it might be a new thought for you to go the other way and put on some pressure offense. In our first two games one year we scored over 100 points, won the games, and the fans loved it. You might get to like it too.

At Michigan State, pressure means a fast break philosophy that keeps the pressure on, not just in normal situations such as the missed shot, but even in the free throw situation where the free throw or basket is made. Here is an explanation of the three phases of our fast break philosophy.

1. Basic Fast Break: This comes after the missed shot (Diagram 1). No. 3 is the logical rebounder, and we want him literally to "explode" out of there by turning, looking and hitting the first receiver he sees. In our system, No. 1 and No. 2 will bring up the ball; they must block out, pay attention to their men, and place themselves in an area to get the long rebound and be in position for the outlet pass. If No. 4 and No. 5 see that they are not in the play because the ball has bounced away from them, they are free to get down the floor as fast as possible; they may even leave their area unguarded.

It is true that you can get the ball up the court faster by a pass than a dribble. But No. 1 should look and not pass if his man is not open. If No. 2 is not open, and he is pressed, he looks to No. 3 for a possible direct pass.

A lot of times, No. 5 will rebound in this situation and the two forwards will be on their way up; thus we will have two quick passes. The key man in this fast break is No. 2. He attempts to draw the pressure from the defense. No. 3 and No. 5 come up in a trailing position, trying to hit a delayed action pass for either a drive in all the way or a shot at the top of the circle.

2. *Missed Free Throw:* This should definitely be a part of the

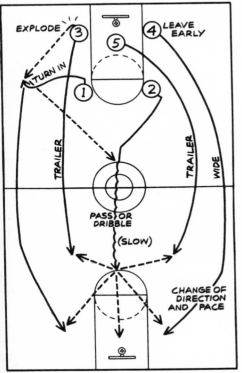

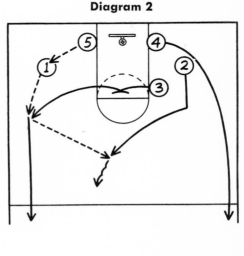

Diagram 1

Diagram 2

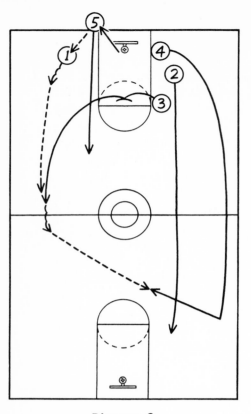

Diagram 3

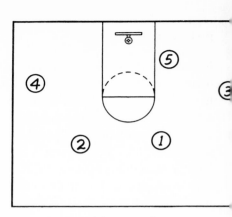

Diagram 4a

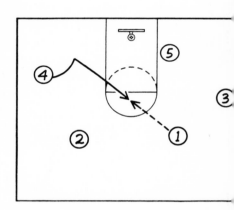

Diagram 4b

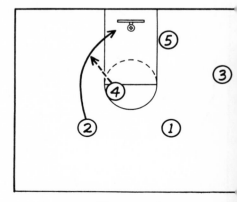

Diagram 4c

fast break (Diagram 2). You don't automatically have the advantage, but you don't give up and bring the ball up slowly. I believe that many defenses loaf between the free throw lines. In our set up, No. 3 takes the shooter; he makes sure the long rebound comes to him. No. 4 and No. 5 are on the defensive part of the line, so they are in a position of advantage for the rebound. No. 1 and No. 2 are on the side in position for an outlet pass.

We sometimes permit No. 4 or No. 5 to tap the ball out to No. 2 if they are sure the defense won't intercept. In the diagram, No. 5 gets the rebound, and passes to No. 1. No. 3 blocks out the shooter. No. 4 takes off on the wing, and No. 2 comes across for the middle pass. No. 1 passes to No. 3 who becomes the other wing man. No. 3 passes to No. 2 for the break. No. 1 and No. 5 become the trailers.

3. Made Free Throw: We feel you can fast break effectively from this situation. The basic pattern is this (Diagram 3): No. 5 (he is right there) quickly takes the made shot out of bounds and passes to No. 1 *immediately*. No. 3, who has blocked the shooter, cuts to the wing and takes the next pass. No. 2 breaks and can continue to the weak side for our "blind pig." No. 4, who has taken off down court, can cut across and get a direct pass from No. 3.

When we use the term "blind pig" it means one of the men on the side of the court sneaks in diagonally toward the free throw lane area while the guard closer to the ball sneaks in behind, either to get the ball back from the forward or make a strong effort for the rebound.) To work our blind pig situation, the break from the made free throw has the men as shown in Diagram 4a.

Normally, the most logical men for No. 1 to pass to are No. 2, No. 3, or No. 5. No. 4, in the corner, doesn't usually expect to get a pass. No. 4 makes a change of direction (Diagram 4b) cutting to the top of the free throw line to get a diagonal pass from No. 1. As he makes his cut, No. 2 sneaks behind his man and cuts for the basket to receive a pass from No. 4 (Diagram 4c). This is based on our experience that the man guarding No. 2 has a tendency to look toward where the ball has gone for a split second, thus giving No. 2 the opportunity to sneak in behind him. Of course, No. 4 might be in a better situation to come up on the blind pig. No. 5 and No. 1 are usually trailers.

If nothing happens, No. 4 has the ball, No. 1 has come down in a safety valve situation, No. 3 is on the side, No. 5 is in the hole where he is supposed to be, and No. 2 and No. 4 merely draw up (No. 4 throws to No. 1 and becomes the weakside man). No. 2 is down in the hole and they make the weakside change and we are ready for our normal offense.

17.

A SIMPLIFIED 1-3-1 OFFENSE

by ED BADGER

Head Basketball Coach
Wright (Chicago, Illinois) Junior College

*Ed Badger has a 76–28 record in four seasons as head basket-
ball coach at Wright Junior College. His teams have won 2
Illinois Junior College conference titles, one runner-up spot
in their regional tournament and 1 Chicago tournament title.*

When I made the transition from coaching in high school to
coaching basketball in junior college, I found out very quickly that
I had to adopt a basic offense that could be used against both zone
and man-to-man defenses—one that was simple to learn because
of the all too frequent turnover of personnel in junior college.

I chose the 1-3-1 tandem offense and modified it to meet our
needs. Diagram 1 shows the basic floor positions in our offense.

O-1 is the quarterback of the offense. He is usually our best ball-
handler, a good driver and jump shooter. O-2 and O-3 are the wing
men. They are our best outside shooters and good drivers. We
usually try to have boys between 6'0" and 6'3" play these positions.
O-4 is our high post man. He is the best outside shooting big man
(usually 6'4" or 6'5"). O-5, the baseline man, is our other big man
who can shoot the short jumper and knows how to drive in.

Side Pattern: The first of our main offensive patterns is called
"side." (Diagram 2.) O-1 passes to O-2 while O-4 screens for O-3

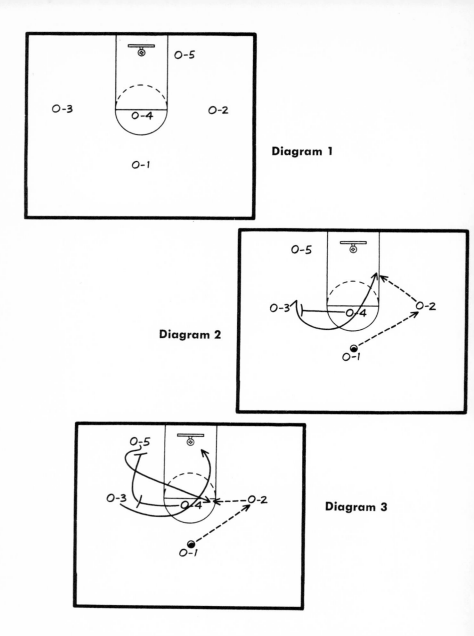

Diagram 1

Diagram 2

Diagram 3

who goes down the middle for the pass from O-2 and the possible lay-up. *Option 1:* O-4 can continue in to screen for O-5 who will attempt a jump shot from the free throw line as in Diagram 3. *Option 2:* O-4 can roll to the basket after screening O-5 (Diagram 4). *Option 3:* If no one is free, O-5 can put an inside screen on for a O-2 jump shot on the free throw line. O-4 and O-3 will hit the

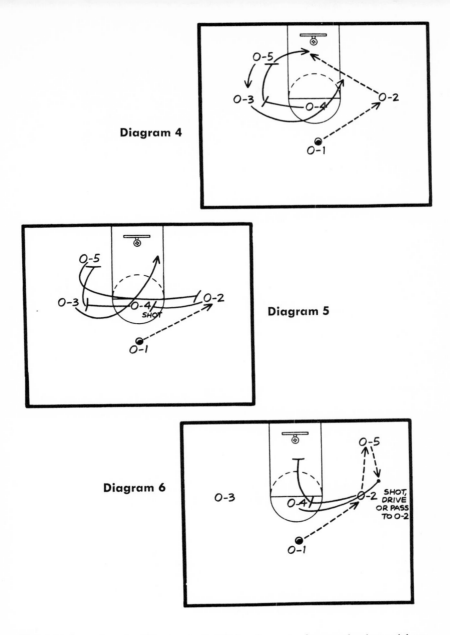

Diagram 4

Diagram 5

Diagram 6

offensive board as in Diagram 5. This play can be worked to either side.

Corner Pattern: This is our second pattern. O-1 passes to O-2 who passes to O-5 and then screens for O-4 who takes a short jump shot or drives if he gets the chance. *Option 1:* After screening for O-4, O-2 rolls to the basket (Diagram 6). *Option 2:* If O-4 is not

127

free for a good shot, he hands off to O-5 and screens for O-3 who has moved to the free throw line. O-2 and O-5 hit the offensive board (Diagram 7). The "corner" can be worked either way.

In our offense, we have used, successfully, these two simple exchanges with our high man O-4 and our baseline man O-5.

The first of these exchanges we call the "change." O-4 changes positions with O-5, and tries to screen O-5's man on the way. O-1

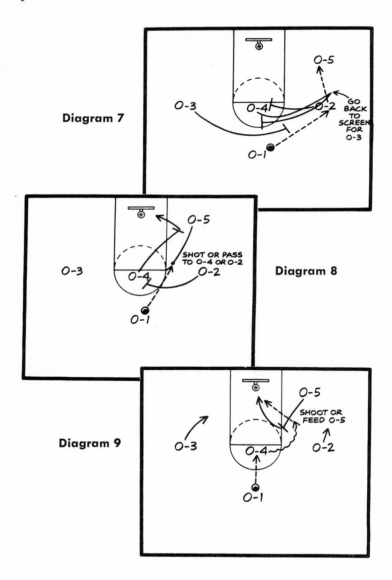

Diagram 7

Diagram 8

Diagram 9

passes to O-5 for the short jump shot, or for a pass to O-4 who rolls after the screen (Diagram 8). Options for this exchange:

- O-2 gets a pass and dribbles over and sets an inside screen for O-3, who takes a jump shot (Diagram 9)
- O-3 screens for O-1 who has a side jump shot; O-4 and O-5 hit the offensive board (Diagram 10)

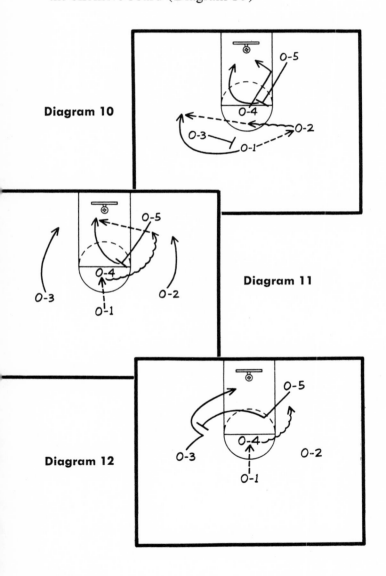

Diagram 10

Diagram 11

Diagram 12

The second exchange we call the "base." We feed O-4 high and have O-5 come up for a screen on O-4's man. O-4 then drives or takes a short jump shot. O-5 rolls to the basket if O-4 is double-teamed. O-2 and O-3 hit the offensive Board (Diagram 11). Options:

- If O-5 does not get the ball, he picks for O-2 and O-3 (depending which side he is on) (Diagram 12).

18.

THE FLASH POST OFFENSE

by HARRY MILLER

Head Basketball Coach
Fresno (California) State College

In his five years at the helm of the Fresno State College basketball teams, Harry Miller has coached them to a 96–40 record. Under Coach Miller's hand, the "Bulldogs" have taken four trips to the NCAA College Division plays-offs and have won four successive California Collegiate Athletic Association conference crowns.

I believe that any effective, well-organized offensive must stress these three things: (1) floor balance and protection against the fast break; (2) fast, simultaneous movement of team members and the ball; and (3) flexibility—offense must be able to cope with all types of man-to-man and zone defenses.

We feel that our flash post offense gives us all three with the important plus value of encouraging a great deal of free-lancing. Here is how it works:

We prefer to put the ball in play with a controlled fast break off the defensive board or with an intercepted pass. If we do not have a fast break opportunity, we set up our flash post which makes up the bulk of our scoring. It is called "flash post" because each member of the squad has an opportunity to play the inside post position depending on the movement of the ball.

We divide our flash post into the following phases: guard-to-center motion; guard-to-guard motion; and guard-to-forward motion.

GUARD-TO-CENTER MOTION

Diagram 1 shows our guard-to-center motion. O-1 makes a direct feed to O-3, and cuts down the right side of the lane for a possible return pass. O-4 executes a close cut off O-1 as O-2 sets his man up for a close cut off O-4. All three cutters are eligible for a return pass. We prefer, however, to get the ball to O-2 who is in the cleared out area where he can go for the drive or jump shot. O-5 comes out to the middle of the court approximately 10 feet behind the free throw circle, directly in line with the basket, for defensive balance.

Diagram 2 shows a variation of our guard-center move. O-1 passes the ball to O-3 and cuts in front or over the top. This is the signal for O-4 to cut sharply along the baseline and for O-2 to set his man up for a close cut off O-1. O-5 rotates out for defensive balance.

Options: O-3 can pass to O-4 moving along the baseline, O-1 cutting hard to basket, or O-2 who is moving into the cleared out section where he is in position to shoot the 17 foot jump shot or drive for the basket.

GUARD-TO-GUARD MOTION

Diagrams 3, 4 and 5 show our guard-to-guard motion. In Diagram 3, O-1 passes to O-2 and immediately makes a lateral move two steps toward O-2. This puts his defensive man in motion and at the same time O-1 is gaining a better cutting angle. O-2 moves the ball to O-5, who has cleared himself on the side with a hard baseline fake. O-5 is then in the "triple threat" position—he may pass, drive or shoot depending on the defensive man's reaction. O-1 now starts a hard, direct cut toward O-3 and goes either right or left of O-3 who screens. We prefer O-1 to go to O-3's right in order to make it more difficult for the defensive man on O-3 to switch. If O-5 does not exercise his shooting or driving options, he looks for O-1. If O-1 does not receive the ball, he moves to the corner and then rotates out for defensive balance.

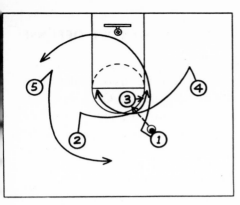

Diagram 1

Diagram 2

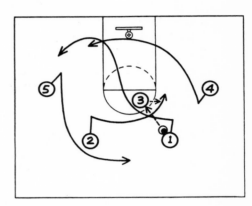

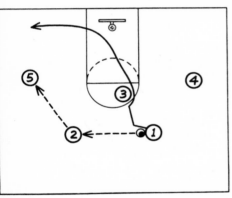

Diagram 3

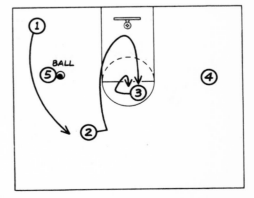

Diagram 4

Diagram 4 illustrates another phase of our guard-to-guard motion. O-2 is watching the action develop on the inside as he fakes away from the ball toward the center of the court. As O-1 clears out, O-2 tries to beat his man with a solo cut down the ball side of the lane looking for a pass from O-5. If he does not receive the pass, he establishes a tight high post position beside O-3 at the free throw line.

In Diagram 5, O-4, who has been watching the play on the strong side, fakes to the baseline and crosses over in front of his man. He must make sure that defense doesn't overplay him as he moves into

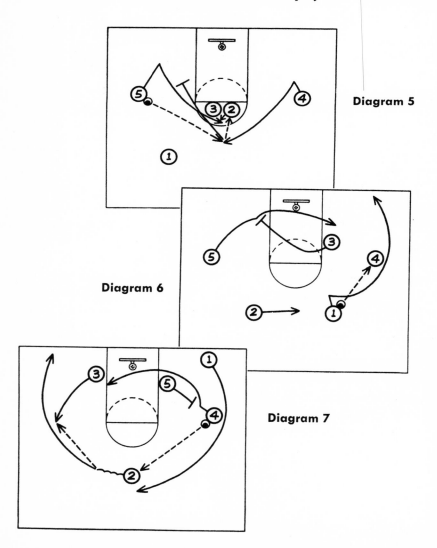

Diagram 5

Diagram 6

Diagram 7

position to receive pass from O-5. O-4 sets up directly in line with the basket 5 feet outside the free throw circle to receive the pass. After he gets the ball, O-4 passes to O-2, O-5 then fakes deep on the baseline in order to set his defensive man up for a screen by O-4. O-5 comes over the top, receiving a pass from O-2 for the jump shot or drive.

GUARD-TO-FORWARD MOTION

We have found the guard-forward move invaluable when we are leading by a few points and are anxious to slow down the tempo and take only the very high percentage shots.

Diagrams 6 and 7 show our guard-to-forward motion. In Diagram 6, O-1 passes to O-4 and follows his pass to a position approximately 15 feet from the basket on the base line. While this is happening, O-2 moves to the middle of the floor and O-3, who originally set up on the ball side, crosses the free throw lane to set a screen on 0-5's man. O-5 then has the option of cutting high or low off the screen. We prefer that he cut low so he can be in the higher percentage shooting area when he receives the ball from O-4. If we do not get the ball after these movements, the continuity is resumed on the left side of the floor after the ball is passed to O-2.

Diagram 7 shows the position of the players after the initial move has been completed. It also shows how we get back to the opposite side of the floor with the ball. O-4 passes the ball out to O-2 who relays it to O-3 (original center now playing forward). O-2 follows the pass and establishes position on the base line approximately 15 feet from the basket. In the meantime, O-5 (original left forward now playing center) sets a screen for O-4 to come in for a low post shot.

We keep this movement going until we earn a good shot in the high percentage area. Should defense choose to apply pressure on the "point guard," we bring the center to a high post for a quick pass and cut the guard being pressured.

19.

STEP PLAY OFFENSE

by Richard E. Baldwin

Head Basketball Coach
Broome Technical (Binghamton, New York) Community
College

Dick Baldwin's 18-year won-and-lost record as head basket-ball coach at Broome Technical Community College is 383–106. This includes 6 Empire State conference titles, 5 Eastern NJCAA regional crowns, and 5 Broome Tech Christmas Classic Championships.

One of the vitally important things that I have learned in my experience in basketball coaching is that the coach *must* adapt his style of play to the type of material he has. And I don't mean minor changes—I mean a major overhaul, if necessary.

The basic aim of *any* offense is to get players into floor positions where they can score. The key to the problem is first to know from where your players can hit best, and then to build an attack that will get them there so that you can get the most mileage out of them. Not only does changing your offense get your players in better hitting position, it also prevents the team's play from getting stereotyped and easily predictable by opposing coaches.

We tried this theory in practice. Our "custom-made" Step Play was originally built around two men—a 6'6" center (O-1 in all diagrams) and a 5'11" corner man (O-2 in diagrams). The center was a poor outside and pivot shooter but was an extremely able and

136

aggressive rebounder. We wanted to keep him near the basket. Our corner man was only 5'11", but was a deadly jump shooter and a good driver. The result: our step play helped us to a 28–3 season. Here is how we worked it:

Our *pivot man* (O-1) lines up at a low post just outside the free throw line with the corner man (O-2) a step or two away from him. The guard (O-3) makes the feed to O-2 and clears. (Diagram 1).

Next, 0-1 takes a step and sets a screen with his back to X-2's side as close as possible without making contact. Since he positions himself within X-2's vision, the screen is perfectly legal. (See Diagram 2 for foot positions.)

As O-2 starts his drive and X-1 starts to switch, O-1 swings his left foot to the rear and towards the baseline to block X-2 out of

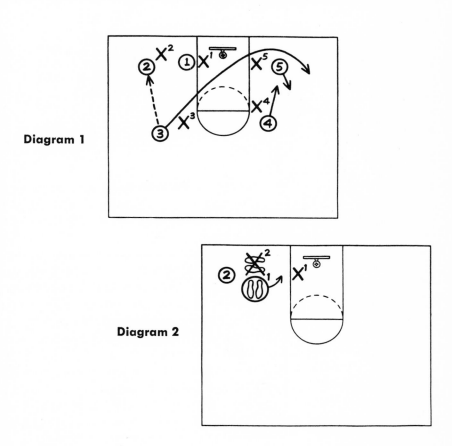

Diagram 1

Diagram 2

the play. O-2 makes a head and shoulder fake to help set up the screen and then drives off O-1's shoulder. (Diagram 3).

Generally, X-1 was forced to switch and O-2 could anticipate going up for the 10 to 15 foot jump shot after about one dribble. Should X-1 switch aggressively, O-1 would roll to the basket for the pass from O-2 and the lay-up.

If X-1 overplays to O-2's inside as in Diagram 4, we have an effective play. O-2 goes to the baseline. This makes it impossible for X-3 (who would sag occasionally and not follow his man) to double team with X-2 on O-1.

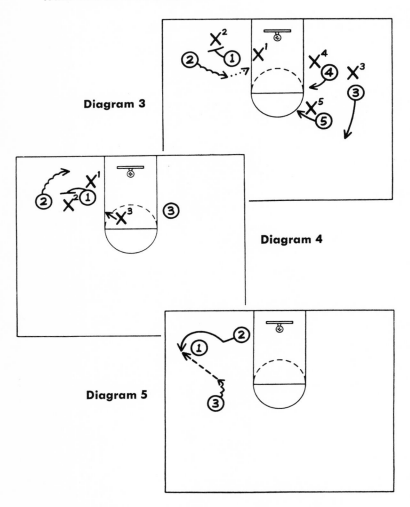

Diagram 3

Diagram 4

Diagram 5

A sag and double team by X-3, X-4, or X-5 is usually avoided simply by the "busy" movements of O-3, O-4, and O-5 shown in Diagrams 1 and 3.

Several teams defensed our step play by forcing O-2 out to the sideline to handle the ball. In this case, when O-1 was unable to set the screen by taking just one step, O-2 would pass to him in the pivot and then cut off him. Also, we would frequently start O-2 in the post position and have him make a quick exchange with O-1 on the side so that he could handle the ball shallow. (Diagram 5.)

20.

THE SINGLE POST OFFENSE

by DICK BUCKRIDGE

Head Basketball Coach
Northwest Missouri State College

In eight years of coaching high school basketball (five at William Chrisman (Independence, Missouri) High School), Dick Buckridge posted a strong 142–46 record and produced 5 conference playoff champion teams. At present, Dick Buckridge is head basketball coach at Northwest Missouri State College.

The single-post offense has been responsible for almost all of the success I have had in basketball coaching. Not only does it produce winning ball clubs, it also allows a boy to take any of the individual free-lance options he is qualified for. It is an offense that has continuity and all options can begin from either side of the floor. A plus value is that it's easy to teach.

Although the single-post is a pattern offense, we never hesitate to shoot the good shot, for example the 12 to 15 foot jump shot. We discourage bad shots by maintaining the confidence that our pattern will produce good ones. We have no rule that states we must take so many passes before we look for a shot—we shoot when the shot is there. Offense is getting the ball through the net.

Here is how I operate the single-post:

BASIC PLAYER ALIGNMENT

Diagram 1 shows the basic distribution of our players. The *guards* penetrate as close to the head of the circle as possible and are from 12 to 15 feet apart. *Forwards* position themselves on an imaginary line from free throw extended and 3 to 4 feet from the sidelines. Our *post-man* works to free himself by moving from the baseline to the free throw line up and down along the lane. He moves to the side where the ball is and this determines our strong and weak sides.

We let our guard with the ball do what his defensive man tells him to. In other words, he moves or operates away from the defensive strength. Aside from giving us a position advantage, this also helps us to control the amount of defensive overplaying. We discourage the guard from making up his mind what to do until defense commits itself.

Five Options: Almost all of our offense consists of the five following options off our basic floor distribution:

1. O-1 makes direct pass to O-5. (Diagram 2) We feel that the old pattern of splitting the post is one of the better maneuvers in basketball. After O-1 passes to O-5, he screens for O-3 who comes over the screen for a jump shot over O-5. If O-3 is not open, O-5 maneuvers for shot or moves ball to O-4 who exchanged places with O-2 on the weak side. O-5 then moves to that side of lane and maintains floor balance.

Diagram 1

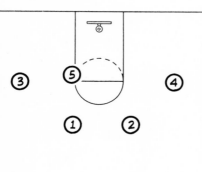

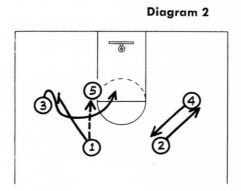

Diagram 2

2. O-1 passes to O-3 and goes outside. (Diagram 3) With this option, we merely split the post from the back side. O-3 returns the ball to O-1 who dribbles to the corner. O-1 then hits O-5 and comes up to screen for O-3.

3. O-1 passes to O-3 and goes inside. (Diagrams 4a and 4b) O-1 passes to O-3 and goes inside. O-3 then dribbles out to O-1 position

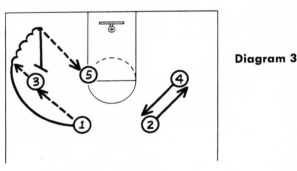

Diagram 3

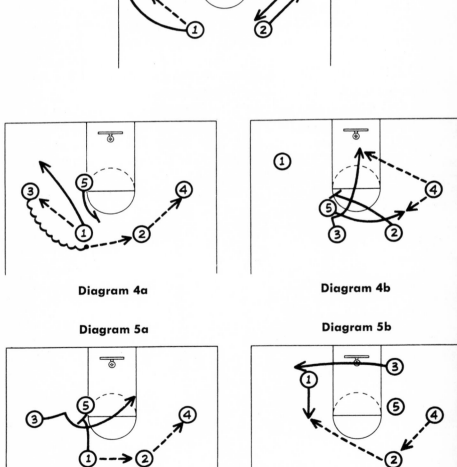

Diagram 4a

Diagram 4b

Diagram 5a

Diagram 5b

and passes cross court to O-2. O-2 passes to O-4 and in the meantime O-5 comes up to screen for O-3 (Diagram 4a). O-3 breaks to basket hoping to get pass from O-4. O-2 then moves to screen for O-5 who can receive pass from O-4 if O-4 is unable to pass to O-3 (Diagram 4b).

4. O-1 passes cross court to O-2. (Diagrams 5a and 5b) O-1 passes to O-2 cross court and then moves to set screen with O-5 for O-3 to break over and receive pass from O-4 who was passed to by O-2 (Diagram 5a). O-5 crosses over O-1 trailing O-3. If O-4 is unable to hit either of these men, he passes to O-2 who may shoot or hit O-1 breaking up on the weak side. O-3 then moves across and may receive pass from O-1 (Diagram 5b).

5. O-1 dribbles toward O-2. (Diagram 6a and 6b) O-1 dribbles toward O-2. O-2 breaks to the basket to prevent the double team. O-1 tries to hit O-2. If this is not possible, he passes to O-4 (Diagram 6a). O-3 comes off the screen set by O-5. If O-4 does not hit O-3, he passes back to O-1. This leaves O-5 on open side of floor to maneuver into a one-on-one situation (Diagram 6b).

In choosing *any* offense for high school, I believe that it is a *must* to adopt one that fits the skills of your players and *stick with it.* Too many coaches change systems as a result of losing two games in a row or having watched some college team use some other offense successfully. Remember, you must allow your boys to adjust to an offensive style before you can expect to get results.

Diagram 6a   **Diagram 6b**

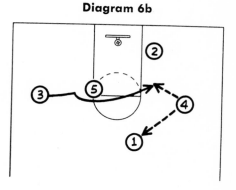

21.

A SUCCESSFUL
OUT-OF-BOUNDS SERIES

by VIC BUBAS
BUCKY WATERS

Head Basketball Coach and
Assistant Basketball Coach
Duke University

The team of Vic Bubas and Bucky Waters have the winning habit at Duke University. The 1962–63 record: 27–3 and third place in the NCAA tournament; 1963–64: 26–5; 1964–65: 29–7 and the Atlantic Coast conference crown. Before joining head coach Vic Bubas as his assistant, Bucky Waters coached the Duke freshmen teams to a 54–11 overall record.

Too often, out-of-bounds plays are given to a team in the final ten minutes of practice before the next game. The reason, of course, is the coach's race against time.

At Duke, we feel that out-of-bounds situations are important and can win games; and the out-of-bounds play under the offensive basket is one of the few situations in basketball where you can predict, exactly, the reaction of the defensive man nearly every time. But we, too, did not want to spend a lot of practice time on the glorification of ten perfectly executed out-of-bounds plays.

We decided on a series of three or four options that were similar in initial deployment, could meet nearly all forms of defense, and were tailored to our personnel. We learned our assignments in pre-season practice and used the plays in all of our scrimmages. By the time December rolled around, we were ready and did not have to confuse our players and take valuable time to learn new plays to meet an expected defense.

Our 1962–63 series are explained here. This, however, is important: The plays were extremely good to us, but it could be that we will never use them again, because they were designed to fit our existing personnel. The following criteria were the basis of our working out our options; the first one is the most important:

1. Suit our personnel.
2. Similarity of initial deployment.
3. Simplicity in purpose and execution.
4. Versatility—with proper diagnosis of the defense by the man taking the ball in bounds, there is an option that will succeed in creating a good scoring opportunity.
5. Easy system of signals.
6. Accessible safety outlets.
7. Offensive board power.
8. Floor balance and defensive responsibility against the fast break.
9. High-quality passer to make the in-bounds pass.

Here are our options:

Option #1 (*Diagram 1*): On overhead slap of the ball, all four men take a quick, long drive step toward the basket. It must be convincing and in unison. This will cause the defense to give ground, and force the slides and chasing of the defense to be more difficult. F-2 goes behind teammates, staying very close and breaks into medium shooting range. If he receives the inbounds pass, he can shoot, feed F-1 in the low post, return pass to G-1 stepping in bounds, or give to G-2 who will balance the floor and run a set offensive pattern.

Simultaneously, F-1, after making his drive step, faces toward the center of the floor to provide a broad screen for F-2. If the defensive man on F-2 is chasing behind the defense, the screen can deter him. If they are switching to cover F-2, or if F-1's defensive man goes out

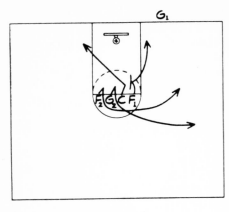

Diagram 1

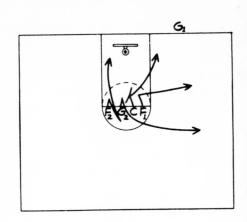

Diagram 2

to pick up F-2, then F-1 will have the next man on his back when he spins and rolls down to the low post.

C cuts through to provide more congestion for the defense to adjust to, and establishes his position on the weak side of the backboard. His move is simultaneous with that of F-1 and F-2 and the path of his cut is very often the deterrent to F-2's defensive man.

G-2 delays two counts and goes to a safe outlet area. If he receives the pass, his first objective is to look for F-1 in the low post or G-1 stepping in bounds.

G-1, after passing, steps in bounds and becomes a threat for a quick jump shot. Many times the out-of-bounds man is not played tightly; in these instances we like to give it right back to him as he steps in bounds for the quick shot.

Option #2 (Diagram 2): On the overhead slap of the ball, all four men make the same drive step. F-2 starts to follow the same cut behind the triple screen, but on the second step, he reverses off his right foot back to the left side of the backboard for a pass or weak side backboard opposition.

F-1 simultaneously fakes to place screen as in Option #1 and plants his left foot and breaks out to medium jump shot area. If he is not open, he has taken a defensive man with him and should allow C to screen and roll to low post with his man behind him.

Simultaneously, C tries to screen the first man to his left with a screen perpendicular to the foul line, and then rolls to the low post on the strong side.

G-1 and G-2 have the same responsibilities as in Option #1.

146

*Option #3 (**Diagram 3**):* (Used against teams that zone the out of bounds play; also a counter maneuver against teams anticipating Options #1 and #2). On the overhead slap of the ball, moves are as follows:

- F-1 breaks directly to the front of the basket.
- C breaks to the weak side of the backboard.
- G-2 breaks out and deep as safety outlet.

F-2 holds for two counts, for these reasons: (a) to provide less congestion, and (b) in the hope that C and F-1 will tie up the defense and sweep the lane clear for the crossfire cut of F-2.

F-2 should go for the lay-up area, but if it is covered, he continues his cut out for the outlet pass.

G-1 has the same responsibility as in Option #1.

*Option #4 (**Diagram 4**):* On the overhead slap of the ball, the four men throw the drive step. G-2 then steps back behind the triple screen as F-2 slides to touch shoulders with C. The in-bounds pass should split C and F-1, and be high and crisp.

G-2 may take the 18-foot shot, or if a defensive man has fought through, he can use F-1 or F-2 as a dribbling screen situation. G-1 will go to the board opposite the penetration of G-2 if he drives, or just go to the offense board if he shoots.

F-1, C, and F-2 will go to form the offensive rebounding triangle if G-2 shoots.

If G-2 drives the opposite side corner man, F-1 or F-2 is responsible to stay back to defend against the fast break. Example: If G-2 drove to his right, F-1 would be working with the screen and roll with him, and F-2 would drift back for defensive balance.

Diagram 3

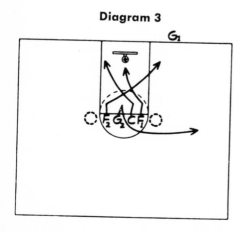

Diagram 4

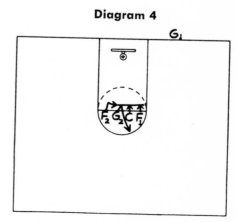

22.

THE FREE THROW

by RON SLAYMAKER

Head Basketball Coach
Roosevelt (Emporia, Kansas) High School

Ron Slaymaker speaks with authority on the "free throw." While playing for Kansas State Teachers College, he was the 1960 NCAA free throw percentage champion, hitting 80 out of 88. Today, as head basketball coach at Roosevelt High School, he holds a five-year record of 81 wins against 28 losses.

Of all the factors determining a win or loss in a basketball game, the "free throw" must rank high. Yet most coaches, due to many reasons, are inconsistent with the emphasis they place on free throwing. The time factor probably heads the list of reasons for these inconsistencies. High school players are intelligent enough to realize the importance of free throwing; but I am sure they often become confused with our up-and-down emphasis of this important phase of the game—often the magic margin between a win and a loss.

At Roosevelt High School, we have the philosophy of emphasis and consistency. I believe in this philosophy because of the success I have had as a player and as a coach in emphasizing free throwing. I know many coaches are doing very well without any organized free-throw practice—but until we fail to see some improvement in our team's charity tosses, we plan to keep on with the emphasis.

200 Throws a Day: If it were not for the time factor in coaching

148

high school basketball, I feel there is no substitute for shooting in excess of 200 free throws a day. Obviously, if one is able to practice a particular skill this many times, some improvement in the skill will be seen. Yet we feel that the psychological gain will far outweigh anything else. If a boy is willing to work to this extent, we know he'll have the feeling that he deserves to be a good free thrower—whether he is or not. Consequently, the gain in his confidence will greatly improve his free throwing.

Style: Taking advantage of what practice time we have, whether it be five minutes, ten or more, we believe that certain fundamentals should be followed. Many young players will lose half of their practice time by shooting their free throws in several different styles—so this is our number one fundamental: we have them adopt one style as quickly as possible and stick with it. In developing a style of free throwing, we never try to change a boy's shooting style—as long as he is successful.

Parallel Stance: We find that the parallel stance with feet spread at shoulder width provides much better balance and allows for a more smooth and even dip. The majority of our players are using this stance with great success. The ball should be held directly in front of the body, a little below eye level, with the wrist slightly cocked. This gives us what we might call a balanced and comfortable pre-shooting position.

Confidence and Concentration: From the pre-shooting position, we call upon our two C's—confidence and concentration. Obviously, there is no place at the free-throw line for any negative thoughts. Confidence can most generally be built through successful experience—which for the majority of us comes only with many hours of dedicated practice.

In the concentration phase is where we perform the rhythmic execution of the shot with a smooth and even dip of the body, an effortless release of the ball, and a follow-through which allows the ball to travel in exactly the same line that it was meant to travel. Without the follow-through, we will get a jerk—and the shot will have little touch.

In younger ball players, there is often a habit that is difficult to break—the dropping of the ball to any place between the chest and waist prior to the shot. As the body takes a slight dip, the ball lowers in relation to the floor, but actually lowers only as far as we have dipped our entire body. The entire execution of the shot should be with the least amount of movement possible. The less the movement of the arms, wrist and body, the less chance there is of making a deviation from a consistent and coordinated shooting form.

When speaking of concentration, we are often asked what we should aim at. We have a simple answer—we aim at the hole. It is said that we should aim at the front rim. If our boys have developed any skill at all, then they will hit just what they aim at; we would rather hit the bottom of the net from the top side than the front rim.

Motivational Devices: Here are a few motivational devices that have helped greatly in our free-throw practice:

1. Blindfold shooting—For the better-than-average free thrower, this is a challenging and beneficial practice. We have the boy shoot with a blindfold placed lightly over the eyes—stressing that the eyes must be kept open for balance. The drill, if practiced consistently, can greatly improve what is called the "kinesthetic" feel.

2. Free-throw charts—These are a necessary item on the locker room wall if you want to measure the progress in practice. For the progress to be meaningful, the circumstances under which you shoot in practice must be similar each day. We have a large bare wall leading into our locker room area where we place in large print the name of each player who has a perfect game at the line. The player with the highest season percentage has his name engraved on an attractive plaque in our trophy case.

3. Small rings—The device or gimmick that has the greatest effect, not only on our free throwing but on our entire basketball program, is the small rings we attach to the inside of our regular goals. These are not to be confused with a rebound goal, because they *do allow* the ball to go through the ring freely, but they require a higher degree of skill than the regular goals.

We have six baskets in our gym, and every basket has a small goal; we never take the goals off except for games. Obviously, the regular goal is no larger than it normally would be—but it appears larger to our players and gives them that little extra bit of confidence we like them to have when they shoot.

We try to be as consistent as we can, but there are times when the free throws aren't falling and we do deviate from the normal. Anything you do differently when they aren't falling will usually result in better shooting. If the shots are falling, we try to leave well enough alone and stick to the usual routine.

To the average person, it may seem that the art of free throwing is somewhat more complicated than it appears to be as we watch a skilled player perform this fundamental shot. It is not until we knit all of the mental and physical aspects into a single, coordinated and effortless shot that we know we have done our best to insure the success of the free throw—often the magic margin between a win and a loss.

PART III

DEFENSIVE TECHNIQUES AND DRILLS

1.

COACHING FUNDAMENTAL DEFENSIVE SKILLS

by JOE LAPCHICK

Head Basketball Coach (Retired)
St. John's University

Joe Lapchick, one of basketball's great names, had been in the game as player and coach for over 50 years. His coaching career at St. John's started in 1936, interrupted from 1947–56 by his stint as head coach of the professional New York Knickerbockers. His college record is 335–129, and his .732 average is fifth among college coaches. Coach Lapchick retired a "winner" at the close of the 1965 basketball season.

The jump shot, and proficiency in shooting it, changed all the traditional ideas of defense. It made a big man out of a small man and made a big man bigger. Today, you can't allow men to stand outside and shoot; you must go out there, play them and pick them up higher.

Traditionally, the ¾ court and half court presses were used when a team was trailing; today teams open up with this defense and apply immediate pressure. The objective: right from the start to force the offense to do things it does not want to do—things it does not normally practice.

Since defense should anticipate and counter offensive moves we should first break offense down into its component parts. It is made up mainly of these basic moves:

- Individual maneuvers such as the one-on-one.
- The play of the pivot man, be it low or high position.
- Two-man screen plays, such as the pass and go behind, pass and go inside, and pass and go away.
- The give and go.

Before going into the various defensive moves to counter the offense, we should discuss, briefly, the five basic component parts which make up the skeleton defense:

1. Stance: The defensive stance should be one of equal balance, weight equally distributed and permitting the player to move easily. It should not be too spread out, as this lessens quick maneuverability.

2. Feet: The "old pros" say defense is played with the feet. It is not too important which foot is forward, but one should be slightly forward. The weight should be on the balls of the feet and not on the heels.

3. Hands: Your hands should be another aid—one hand should be up and the other down—they should not be too extended as they tend to force you off balance. On jabbing, slap up, rather than down. On blocking shots, make sure you go straight up—forcing the shooter to extend himself rather than bringing the hand down and fouling the shooter.

4. Eyes: In the old days, we played our own man nose to nose; today, we are away from the ball. We try to place ourselves so we can see both our man and the ball at the same time. In playing the man with the ball, this means an effort to use split vision to avoid being picked off. This brings us to consider the use of VOICE.

5. Voice: Calls should be loud and clear so as to warn teammates of impending screens. Don't deliver a soliloquy—sound off in simple calls like—SWITCH—STAY—etc.

TECHNIQUES AND DRILLS

Our plan at St. John's is to break our maneuvers into drills we practice daily. Here are some of the techniques or drills, designed to put defensive pressure on the basic offensive moves.

No. 1—One-on-one: We break the squad down into pairs, one man taking offense, the other defense. The offensive man is free to fake, drive and to use jump shots. After five attempts, the defense becomes the offense and vice-versa. We stress here the defense should be active rather than passive—by jabbing at the offense, it keeps them off balance.

Point 1: We emphasize that on the *FAKE* drive, our first move is backward with both feet. Then we slowly approach the offensive man and set the pace again (Diagram 1a). Never lunge at the driver so as to become vulnerable to fake shot and drive.

Point 2: On the drive—as the driver approaches the basket—he should close the gap, looking to draw the charge. Watch for the change off the dribble.

The one-on-one moves should be practiced from the various parts of the court—with specific instruction applied to each area, such as protecting the baseline (Diagram 1b)—or forcing the dribbler to the sidelines (Diagram 1c). Make sure the shooter is checked on all

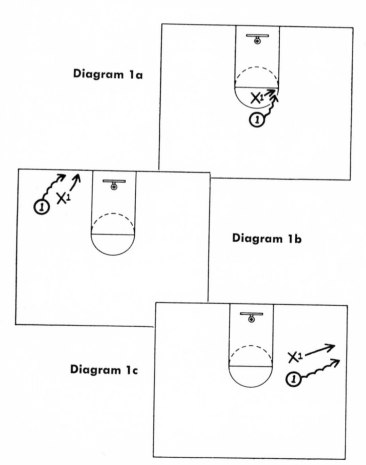

Diagram 1a

Diagram 1b

Diagram 1c

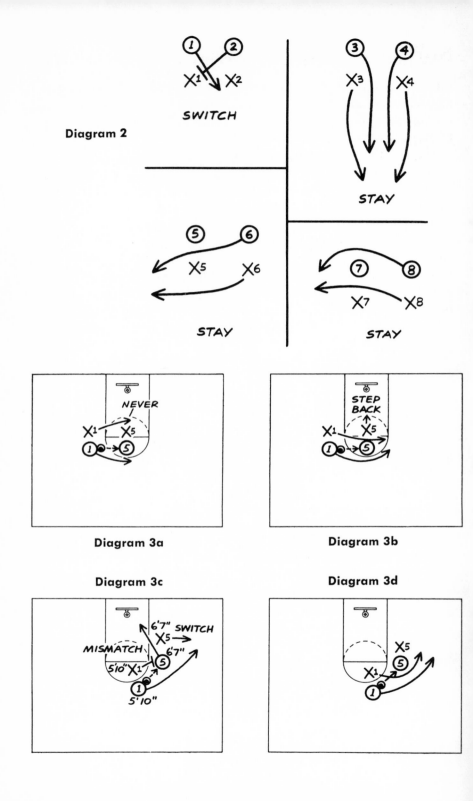

Diagram 2

SWITCH

STAY

STAY

STAY

NEVER

Diagram 3a

STEP BACK

Diagram 3b

Diagram 3c

MISMATCH   6'7" SWITCH

5'10"

Diagram 3d

shots so as to prevent follow-up shots. The purpose, of course, is to stop baseline and sideline drives. You stop the baseline drive by forcing the driver into the pack; the sideline drive by forcing a lateral movement where the sideline is an ally.

No. 2—Two-on-two (Switch and Stay): When I first started coaching I noticed that many times my players were either picked off or two men would wind up covering one man while one offensive man would be free. The reason was that my boys would not talk, and when they did, they would utter "I got him"—a rather nebulous, indecisive and not very clear expression. So, we insist that two words—"SWITCH" and "STAY," and only these two words—be used. Our drill breaks the team into groups of four—two defensive players line up opposite two offensive players without the ball (Diagram 2). The offensive players attempt to run the defensive players into each other and free themselves. The defensive players use two terms "switch" and "stay" to try and stay with their men. BACK man calls the switch as he has a better view of what is happening. If he thinks his man can fight his way through, he calls "stay." When the players reach the opposite side of the court, they reverse position, then the offense becomes defense and vice-versa.

No. 3—(Post Play): Many teams use the "post" play—usually at the foul line, or the foul line extended. We work our drills to avoid the following situations:

1. Going behind your teammate (Diagram 3a). Sometimes he can go between, but rarely (Diagram 3b).

2. Getting picked off.

3. Causing a mismatch where your guards wind up playing taller forwards and centers (Diagram 3c).

The significant thing about this move is one of anticipation. We must try to fight our way over the top so as to stay with our man (Diagram 3d). Never go behind our teammate because that leaves our opponent unguarded. Our teammate who is playing the "post" man, can help by letting us know of the impending block and by stepping back (Diagram 3b) and letting us through if we are stuck —and thirdly we should be ready to switch but only as the last resort, and when absolutely necessary.

No. 4—(Pivot Play): Essentially, the problems concerned with the movement of the pivot are stopping the pivot from scoring; or

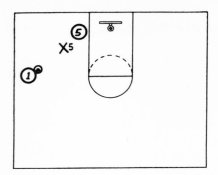

Diagram 4a

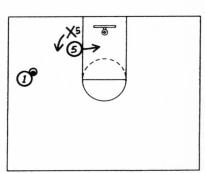

Diagram 4b

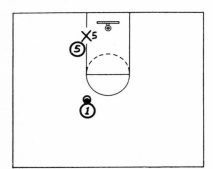

Diagram 4c

Diagram 4d

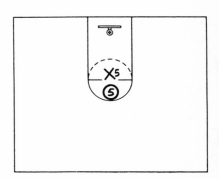

at least lessening his powers or preventing the plays coming off the pivot such as the crisscross. There are certain specifics which can be applied:

    a. Fronting the pivot man in a low pivot—that is preventing him from getting the ball by playing in front of him (Diagram 4a). The possibility of the "dummy" pass is not his responsibility, but rather the weak side forward.

    b. In a medium pivot, the defense should play the strong side, that is, the side where the ball is being passed. For example, if the pass is coming from the corner, our play is to force him into the lanes (Diagram 4-b), and if the pass is coming from the center of the court, overplay and force him baseline (Diagram 4-c).

    c. On the high pivot, we should play behind and drop off, so as to avoid fouling him once he gets the ball, and at the same time, be able to pick up cutters coming off him (Diagram 4-d). Unless he is a good shot, drop him a foot or two and make sure he checks out on all shots.

2.

PRINCIPLES OF SOUND BASKETBALL DEFENSE

by Lou LaGrand

Head Basketball Coach
Potsdam (New York) State College

The 1962–63 basketball season was the best one in the history of Potsdam State College. Coach Lou LaGrand led his team through a 16-game winning streak to a 19–3 season and took them all the way for the school's first New York State University Championship. And that's not all: Potsdam was second defensive team in the nation with a 45.9 average. The last two seasons his squads compiled a 25–15 mark, for an overall three-year record of 44–18.

Basketball is a game full of variables. The only phase of the sport that is relatively stable and can bring consistent success is, I feel, a sound, aggressive and dedicated defense. This is the type of defense we have here at Potsdam.

Our basic aim is, of course, to prevent the offensive team from doing what it wants to.

Don't kid yourself. Defense definitely *is not* a glamorous part of basketball. And anything you can do in the way of putting up bulletin boards, posting comparative defensive statistics, and otherwise giving defensive performance the recognition it deserves will be absolutely necessary.

162

Here are some principles and techniques that have been responsible for our defensive success:

1. Call Out: One of the intangibles of a successful defense is how well teammates communicate with each other on the court. Players must "call out" to alert each other of imminent screening situations, especially the blind or back screen. Once warned, players can take evasive action in order to reverse switching situations. We also emphasize the need to talk in the following instances: a) calling out a high post; b) encouraging a teammate to stay with his man; c) letting a teammate know that there is help available if he forces his man into a certain area; d) if a man guarded breaks loose; and e) on fast break coverage.

2. Forcing: Next to picking up at the half-court line, forcing is our front line of defense, and therefore probably the single most important defensive technique to master. Proper execution of forcing stance (which is unlike the normal guarding stance) can force the man being guarded to move out of a certain area to receive the ball. The stance consists of the defensive player assuming a bent knee position, with the same arm and leg in front of opponent, while leading the opponent's movement toward the ball. The arm is extended with the palm toward the passing lane.

Diagram 1 shows the aproximate position for contesting the pass. The reverse must be guarded against. Many offenses begin with the pass to the forward. This is the action that must be forced out and away from the basket. *Never allow any offensive man to receive a pass inside foul line distance* (15 feet). This same forcing maneuver is used by all players, regardless of size and position played.

3. Open Up—Get the Angle: This principle refers to getting away from an offensive man that does not have the ball. It is the key

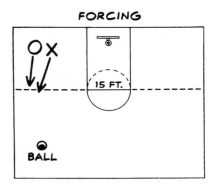

FORCING

15 FT.

BALL

Diagram 1

GETTING THE ANGLE (FORWARD)

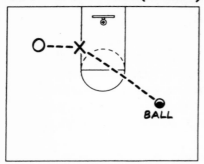

Diagram 2

GETTING THE ANGLE (GUARD)

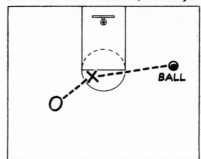

Diagram 2a

BEATING ACROSS

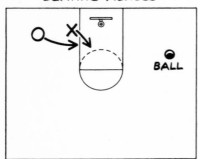

Diagram 3

BEATING TO A POST

Diagram 4

Diagram 5

STOPPING BASELINE DRIVE

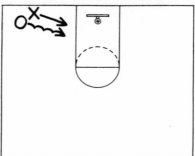

to strong defensive play and demands that the defender have both the ball and his man in sight (good peripheral vision is a must). The technique of opening up and getting the angle is most useful in helping out a teammate guarding the ball handler, preventing screening and defending against roll-ins or cutters looking to receive a pass. Diagrams 2 and 2a show the forward and guard respectively opening up and getting the angle to see both the man they are guarding and the ball.

4. *Beating Across:* This action is aimed at taking away all passes to a player cutting across court for the ball and a possible drive to score. It is used mainly against a team running the Auburn shuffle and on weak-side screens for forwards. Again, the extended arm plays an important role in discouraging and preventing pass-ins. The defender must position himself in relation to the ball in order to beat his opponent to the area or driving lane where it could be received. (Diagram 3) Defender assumes the bent knee position with weight low, enabling him to make a quick start as the offensive man begins to move.

5. *Beating to a Post:* In this move, the defender, alerted to the presence of a post man, pressures the opponent cutting off the post to alter his path. This allows a defensive man to squeeze through between the post and the cutter. It makes it unnecessary to call the switch and also stops the chance of the uncontested jump shot behind the post. What we really would like to do is have the defensive man force the reverse and stop the normal offensive action. Occasionally the reverse may work, but usually defensive help is available from teammates guarding baseline opponents. Diagram 4 shows a guard forcing his opponent above the post. The same technique is used on cuts off the low post. The maneuver is also referred to as "going over the top."

6. *Never Give the Baseline:* We feel that when an opponent drives the baseline and gets by his defensive man, his shot will be uncontested. We know, however, that if we assume an initial position which allows only the drive to the middle, help will be near in case the dribbler gets by the defensive man. (Diagram 5) Here, we use a belly-baseline stance in which the inside leg of the defender (the leg closest to the half-court line) is lined up with the crotch of the offensive man. In this way, the defense is overbalanced to the baseline, yet in strong position to stop the drive to the middle. This is also our normal guarding stance in the one-on-one situation.

7. A Hand in the Face on All Shots: The psychological effect of close guarding is an important factor in destroying shot-making consistency. We insist that *every* time an opponent shoots—even if he is 40 feet from the basket—the defensive man must get a hand up to disconcert the shooter. The flicker of fingers in front of the "shooting eye" of an opponent can often cause a mental flinch or tightening up and result in a missed field goal. Make no mistake. This is energy-consuming work, but the cumulative effect on shooting percentages is amazing and is proof that each player is staying with his opponent and playing an aggressive game.

8. Block Out—Especially the Shooter: It has often been said that "the backboards are the backbone of basketball." And it is well known that full control of the boards wins most games. We spend a considerable amount of time toughening up our rebounders through a drill made popular by N.Y.U.'s Lou Rossini. Here is how it works:

The entire team is placed under the basket. Pushing, shoving and hacking are allowed, but no dribbling. The player who scores three baskets first is the winner. The beauty of the drill is that, properly controlled, it gives each player the feeling of handling and shooting the ball under extreme pressure. It also increases their ability to retrieve the ball despite the body contact which is always present in rebounding.

9. Reminders: We also use conventional rebound drills and others where blocking out the shooter is stressed. The shooter must *never* be allowed to follow his shot, recover it, and shoot again. Here are our rebound reminders:

- The rebounding area is the "football field" of the basketball court. It's rough. Much body contact is to be expected. Those who shy away are not playing a normal aggressive game.
- Aggressive board work nullifies the second and third shot attempts and consequently decreases the other team's point totals.
- Box-outs should be made as far from the basket as possible. Keep the opponent away from the bucket. This will heighten the possibilities for receptions on hard bouncing rebounds.

3.

DEFENSIVE FUNDAMENTALS AND DRILLS

by Fred "Tex" Winter

Head Basketball Coach
Kansas State University

Fred "Tex" Winter, who guided the 1963–64 Wildcat team to a 22–7 record, its seventh Big Eight crown in the past nine seasons, and the Midwest NCAA championship, now has totaled 200 wins over 11 seasons at Kansas State. He is the winningest coach in KSU basketball history. In fact, Coach Winter never has had a losing season at Kansas State since he took over the head coach job in 1953.

Attend a basketball coaching school or get into a "bull session" on basketball and the talk invariably centers around the offensive aspect of the game. It's fun to talk offense and coach offensive patterns to your team. Players enjoy that phase of the game, and fans always follow the man with the ball. Despite this emphasis, the good defensive teams are the ones that win the championships.

Kansas State University has won the Big 8 conference championship seven of the last nine years. Each of these championship teams were outstanding defensive clubs. Even though our teams have received publicity on our "triple post offense," I would be the first to say that our defensive ability accounts for our outstanding record. This being the case, here are some of my thoughts on defensive basketball:

167

DEFENSIVE FUNDAMENTALS

• *Individual Defensive Ability:* Individual defensive technique is the basis on which any sound team defense is built. Therefore, it's imperative that much time be spent on the development of sound individual defensive ability. This ability is based on the player's mental as well as his physical capabilities. He must be inculcated to do a great job on the man he is covering. A burning desire and a great pride in doing the job defensively will cover up a multitude of defensive errors—because in the final analysis, good defensive play is as much a matter of hustle, desire and pride as it is anything else.

Our players are aware that everything else being equal, the player who can play the better defense will get the nod. We like to say that we pick our team on the basis of their defensive abilities—and I believe, everything considered, we do.

• *Individual Defensive Footwork:* We teach a basic individual defensive footwork to our players, depending on the location of the ball on the court and the offensive player's strengths and weaknesses (information obtained by scouting). Any time the player with the ball is in a position from opposite the top of the circle to the corner, we will play in such a manner that we force him to the inside. In other words, we try to take the base line drive away from him by forcing him back into the congested area of the middle.

In order to accomplish this objective, we "over-play" the base line in one of two ways. We either play in a stance position with the base line leg back, or we overshift one-half man to the base line side.

We feel that a good defensive player can cover individually with either foot forward; therefore, we do not insist on a certain foot forward on one side of the floor, etc. We tell our players that they must learn to play defense when covering a man on the side of the court with either foot forward in a stride stance; and to protect the base line accordingly. That is, if the base line leg is up, then you must over-play the base line side one-half man—and if the base line leg is back, you must split the defensive man down the middle with your front leg.

• *Close Out or Approach:* Probably the most important aspect of individual defensive play is the "close out" or "approach." No one can cover a good offensive player, one on one, who is not ready to do so *as* or *before* the offensive player receives the ball. This makes it imperative for the defensive man to react to the ball on every pass that is made, and particularly to the pass about to be received or intended for the man he is covering. Unless the defensive man reacts properly and *closes out on the pass—or before the pass is made,* it is impossible to do a good job of defense on the assigned man. The close out is made in such a manner that the defensive man is ready to play defense on the offensive man *as* he receives the ball—or *before* he receives it if inside the 15 foot shooting area. This approach to the ball should be made in a "step-drag action" with the advanced foot moving forward first and then the back foot in a boxer's type shuffling of the feet.

  • *Retreat or Loosening Action:* Any loosening or retreating action necessary is done by moving the rear foot back first. In other words, we always try to *advance with our front foot first* and *retreat with our rear foot first.* In this manner we can avoid the cardinal defensive sin of crossing our legs on the close out or retreat. We do not use the "drop step" (front foot drops rapidly back to position behind the rear foot) until *after* the loosening step with the rear foot is made. Avoiding the immediate use of the drop step enables us to reapproach the man with the ball with the same foot forward initially used.

  The loosening action is always used on any initial fakes or moves by the offensive man—and the drop step is made on any subsequent moves by the offensive man that goes to the advanced foot side of the defensive player.

  • *Getting in Motion with Man:* Once the offensive man has made his move on the dribble, we want our defensive men to be in a position well advanced of the dribbler. The defensive man stays low and he does not attempt to play the ball until he is in a good position to do so. He must stay in motion with the dribbler in such a manner as to be able *to play the dribble, as it comes off the floor, with the inside (close) hand.* Never do we want to go after the ball with the outside hand, because in doing so it is impossible to stay ahead of the dribbler. The feet must be moved with nimbleness and quickness in a shuffling, boxer's type action. We attempt to force the dribbler to change his direction by an aggressive over-play in the path of the direction he is attempting to go. We want a constant pressure exerted on the dribbler, forcing him in another direction.

DEFENSIVE DRILLS

• *Mass Defensive Footwork Drills:* A mass defensive footwork drill is used each day in our freshman practice sessions. The drill lasts from 5 to 10 minutes and is designed to give the players practice moving the feet rapidly. It teaches body balance, stance, proper footwork technique in executing the approach, retreat, getting in motion, etc. It is also a great conditioning drill and is used by individual players the year round. (Diagram 1.) In this drill, the stance, retreat step and getting in motion can be checked and practiced. The players line up with their *backs* to the coach. On the whistle, the players execute the "drop step" and shuffling action of the getting in motion process.

Diagram 2 illustrates the approach and retreat phase of the drill. It is set up the same as shown in Diagram 1 except the players *face* the coach. The stance is checked closely and then on the whistle, the players close out or approach in a shuffling action—always approaching with the front foot first in a boxer's type footwork. On the second whistle, the players stop their approach and immediately see how fast they can take the "drop step" in a retreating action.

• *One on One Drill:* The one on one teaches good individual defensive and offensive footwork, and is one of our most used drills in early season practice sessions. Note in Diagram 3 that we incorporate the third man in this drill; thus, enabling us to practice the vital "close out" aspect of our individual defensive footwork. This third man also provides us with an opportunity to work offensively on one of the most important passes in our style of play—the guard to forward pass.

The inclusion of the guard–forward pass simulates more closely the "game-like" situation under which the players must learn to properly react instinctively. *Execution:* [1] plays defense on ②. ① advances the ball from back court to forecourt. ② influences his defensive man [1] by stepping toward the basket. As ① reaches a position approximately 15 foot distance ② receives the ball in such a manner that his body is placed between the defensive man [1] and the basketball. [1] "close out" on the pass so that he is ready to play

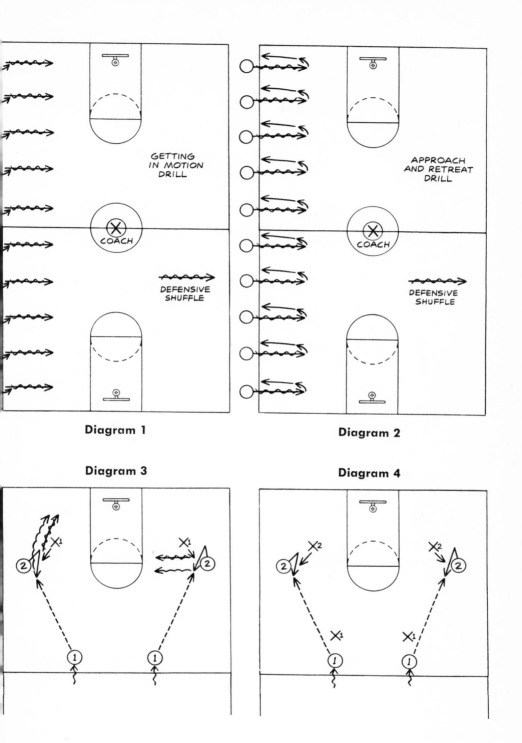

Diagram 1

GETTING
IN MOTION
DRILL

COACH

⌇⌇⌇→ DEFENSIVE
SHUFFLE

Diagram 2

APPROACH
AND RETREAT
DRILL

COACH

⌇⌇⌇→ DEFENSIVE
SHUFFLE

Diagram 3

Diagram 4

defensive on his man, ②, as ② receives the pass. (Before ② receives the pass in a pressing type defense.)

• *Two on Two Drill:* Following a progressive order, we next use a two on two drill as illustrated in Diagram 4. This drill includes the defensive man on the guard, as well as the forward. All two man (guard and forward) situations are reviewed and practiced through this drill. We defense these situations by rules, and it is through drills such as this one that we learn to react instinctively to all possible offensive situations. We leave nothing to chance, and are convinced that it is not so much the method used in defensing, but rather that you have a definite method and practice it until it becomes automatic.

We continue to build our defense (as well as our offense) in progressive steps: three on three drill (using the centers as the third man); four on four (two guards and two forwards), etc., until we are ready for five on five play.

4.

TIPS ON INDIVIDUAL DEFENSIVE PLAY

by SLATS GILL

Head Basketball Coach
Oregon State University

Amory T. (Slats) Gill is a true veteran of the basketball wars. He has been head coach at Oregon State University for 35 years and has won 575 games and lost 388 in that period —which makes him one of the winningest coaches in the game. He retired at the close of the 1964–65 season.

Don't believe the old saying that a good offense is the best defense. A good offense is a good offense; a good defense is a good defense. The key is this: When two equally good offensive teams play each other, the loser is the one with defects in its defense.

We take pride in our defense at Oregon State. Here are some of our thoughts on defensive play:

1. When a team is jumping over a post, we believe it is better to move behind the post when the ball is not involved than to move outside the post. We make the man who is guarding a specific opponent responsible for his shots over the post. If a switch comes, it comes when the offensive man drives by the post, either with or without the ball.

2. We use a technique called "tagging through" a screen in certain situations. It is particularly important against a deep inside screen where the screener may fake and cut to the basket in case a changing defense is used.

173

174 TIPS ON INDIVIDUAL DEFENSIVE PLAY

It is impossible for a defense to change men fast enough against a deep screen to stop a shot over the head of the screener. If the switch is made fast enough to block the overhead shot, a fake screen and cut to the basket makes the play very effective.

In order to handle this situation, we "tag through" the screen. By this we mean that the defensive man avoids the screen by moving out of defensive position and running directly behind his man in the same straight line or arc made by the offensive man; in effect, allowing him to run interference. The defensive man's main effort is to regain position after avoiding the screen by tagging through it.

3. A key responsibility of the coach is the assignment of a defensive man against an opponent's star player. Here are some points:

- Our defensive man concentrates on the first offensive move of his man, perhaps overplaying it, and the second move is taken by the team or action of the other four.
- We keep our defensive man outside the post as the offensive man moves to position *with* the ball.
- In most cases it is possible to keep the defensive man behind the post when the offensive man goes outside *without* the ball. We do not make any changes in switching our defense on the man going outside in this situation. If he takes his position and then drives by, we switch as he makes his move by the post to the basket.
- It is important to tag through on any deep inside screen so that it is not necessary to make a switch, as the offensive man moves away from the end line. It is a defensive problem to try to switch or change men when the ball is not involved, so we try to sag and move through screens on the weak side.
- Many coaches feel a defensive man should move with a boxer step at all times. We think he should turn and run if he is in difficulty.
- On the cutaway or roll, we either switch and move up to play in between the ball and the man on his cut, or we sag with our deep man who momentarily plays a zone until play slows. If none of these methods is successful, we send a third man in to stop a man rolling through the middle, and sag our other two men as fast as possible.

4. Defense for the forward-to-forward, or reverse action, offense is important. "Forward-to-forward" is a term used in the West—and perhaps elsewhere—to designate the offense that has a forward on the weak side cutting by the center who is moving toward him and away from the ball.

The main precaution here is to be in position according to the distance of the ball from the man the defensive player is guarding.

- If the ball is on the opposite sideline, the defense can be very loose, but as the ball moves back to the point, the defensive men should take a tighter position. Against this offensive pattern we try very hard not to switch because it makes the defense very vulnerable to the "backout" for the center (the "backout" is the fake screen by the center who moves away from the basket during interval of the switch of the two defensive men involved).

5. Defense usually has to play strength against strength, and there are ways to help on the post man.

- Play behind him, checking him away from the board and allowing the guards to sag to help on any passes to the post.
- Play the forwards loose, discouraging passing into the center. Play the defensive man ahead of the center and sag from the weak side so the overhead pass will be taken by the guard off the weak side forward. It is important that the post defensive man keep his man between himself and the teammate helping him.

6. When playing a star, it is important to overplay his best move. You cannot get help if he shoots over your head, so you must play over the top. Play him toward your help.

7. Play a give and go by dropping away toward the ball. The natural defensive maneuver against a give and go is for the defensive men to give ground away from the cutter directly toward the basket. If it is handled in this manner, the defense is very vulnerable. The proper defensive maneuver is not only to give ground on the pass, but to give ground toward the ball and retain position on the offensive man on the side toward the ball; this necessitates the pass being made over the head of the defensive man to the cutter.

5.

TIPS ON
MAN-TO-MAN DEFENSE

by JAMES C. McLEOD

Head Basketball Coach
Hickman (Columbia, Missouri) High School

James McLeod's 15-year basketball coaching record is 219–72. He has been head basketball coach at Hickman High School for the last six years. His record there: 121–34; 9 invitational tournament wins; 3 conference championships and 2 regional crowns.

I believe that the man-to-man defense is the best one for basketball. It is adaptable to *all* types of offense and isn't so hard to teach as is so often believed. At Hickman, we use a pressure man-to-man defense. Here are the cardinal points:

Attitude: The most important thing in a man-to-man defense is the attitude of each individual on the squad. He must be made to realize the importance of defense to the overall basketball picture.

Trying to sell a high school boy on defensive basketball is no easy job. Players, especially young players, like to see their names in print. And the papers print the scorers, not the defenders. Still, the coach *must* sell defense. In our situation, the main selling job is done for us. The basketball program in our school system begins in the seventh grade. Although the program has no direct connection with us, we are lucky in that the junior high school coaches instill the correct attitude for playing defense in the boys early in their basketball careers. Although you may not have a junior high system like ours, the idea is still the same—the right attitude for playing defense *must* be instilled in boys as early as possible.

Pressure: I believe that most offenses are only one, two or three man offenses—that is, only one, two or three men are directly involved at the point of attack while the other men have only secondary duties. For this reason, our team defense is designed to apply pressure on the men involved and to let the rest of our men drop off and remain ready to give assistance if it is needed.

We like to apply pressure to the man with the ball and the next logical receivers *at all times.* We want to force the man to do something other than what he wants to do—to make him use his second or third choice. If a dribbler wants to dribble to the sideline, we force him to go to the middle. If a cutter wants to go around the ball, we force him to go away from it or make a wide circle. This is "making the opposition run their offense left handed."

Confusion: Confusion is the defensive man's worst enemy. We practice against each offensive maneuver in the way we think it will happen on game night. We leave nothing to chance—each player must know how to handle each individual move an opposing player may make. He must know how to defense his man when he has the ball and when he does not. He knows that when the offensive man has the ball he can fake, dribble, shoot or pass; and when he doesn't have the ball he can cut, receive, or play the weak side. Our men are drilled to handle each of these situations.

Recognize Shooting Position: A defensive player must know when his opponent has the ball in shooting position, and must know how to react. If the offensive man has the ball below his chest, it is very difficult for him to shoot. In this case, we coach our boys to slide back a step. If the man brings the ball above his chest, the defender slides forward. If he fakes toward our front foot, we drop it back as we slide away. If he fakes toward our back foot, we merely slide away. If he fakes a shot, we tighten up. We impress upon our players the importance of having good balance at all times. We tell them that they must never jump until the opponent leaves the ground—you cannot play defense in the air.

Overplay the Dribbler: We try to force the dribbler away from the basket by overplaying and putting extreme pressure on him. We want the dribbler to move across the court, so we instruct our defensive man to overplay to the point of straddling the ball. The dribbler will then have to veer out, reverse, or dribble across in front of the defensive man. If he veers out, we have upset his offense by making him go wide and away from the basket. When he reverses, we can get back to cover him going the opposite direction. Anytime a man reverses, we drop off one step. We do not want him to drop step and pinch out our defensive man. It takes a very clever dribbler to cross over in front of a defensive man applying pressure without having the ball tied up, intercepted, or batted away.

Harass the Shooter: The defensive man must keep the shooter from concentrating on his shot. The best defense against any shooter is to keep him from getting his favorite type of shot from his favorite spot. Defense must force him into the low percentage areas and not allow him to handle the ball in the high ones.

Harass the Passer: We try to get the passer so rattled that he throws a quick or inaccurate pass that can be intercepted. At the same time, we are playing the receiver in order to close the passing lane and upset the timing between the two. The man covering the receiver must always be alert to prevent the cut and feed behind him. After the passer releases the ball, the defensive man should drop off slightly and move a step in the direction of the pass. By this, we hope to force the cutter to make a wide circle on the outside screen or force him to cut back and make it difficult for him to set the inside screen.

Defensing the Screen: I believe that screening situations are the most difficult things to defense because of the varying judgment of officials. Decisions range from not allowing a defensive man to touch the screen to letting him knock down the screener as long as he stops and does not go through.

On outside screens away from the scoring area, we slide through. In the scoring area, we try to go over the top. If this is impossible, we switch.

On inside screens, we try to force the offensive man away so he cannot set the screen. If, however, he does set the screen, the man covering him must let his teammate know it is there. We use the signal "STOP"—the man being screened can usually tell where the sound is coming from so he knows where the screen is set. When he hears the signal, he drops the foot toward the screener back and outside the screen. If the offensive man drives off the screen, the switch is automatic—the two defensive men have no choice. They know who will have each man regardless of what happens. The switch is very aggressive to make him pick up the dribble immediately.

Defensing Post Splitting: This is another very difficult offensive maneuver to defend against. We do not want to be forced back inside or behind the post man. Our defensive men try to meet in front of the post and make the switch. If they do not meet, there is no switch. The post man is responsible for any free man.

6.

SOME THOUGHTS ON THE ZONE PRESS

by HARRY KINERT

Head Basketball Coach
River Forest (Oak Park, Illinois) High School

Harry Kinert moved to his present position as head basketball coach at River Forest High School after coaching three successive state finalists at Freeport (Illinois) High School. Coach Kinert's over-all record to date is 299 wins against 188 losses.

I regard the zone press as a gambling defense—if it works, fine; if not it was worth the try. I'd rather try to win and get beat by ten or twelve points than play it cool without any chance to win. I tell my players this: Against a zone press the opponents may get three to six easy baskets a game, BUT if the press is well executed it should double that number of points by interceptions and easy layups.

That first interception is important psychologically; since the defense is a gambling defense, you have to be daring.

I like the zone press (we use a 1-2-2 which I'll outline in a moment) for these reasons:

- Even if the press is broken, in many cases the opponents will be upset and their shooting will be below par.
- Many teams are coached to slow up and set up when they reach

mid-court; you can press and they will wait for you to set up the defense. What more can you ask?

- The zone press is the easiest way to get your opponent to play your type of game.
- Just because the opposition handles the ball well is no reason why they cannot be zone pressed effectively.

Our general set up is shown in Diagram 1 (O indicates offensive players, X defensive players). We use this positioning no matter where the offense places their men. X-1 is the key man. He is usually our tallest man and is placed here for these two reasons:

1. He is usually closest to the basket and in good position to put heat on the throw-in quickly.
2. By crowding the end line he makes the long pass almost impossible.

Diagram 1

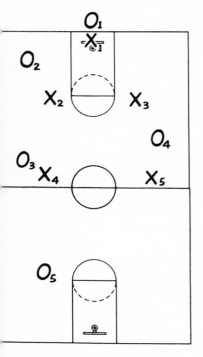

Diagram 2

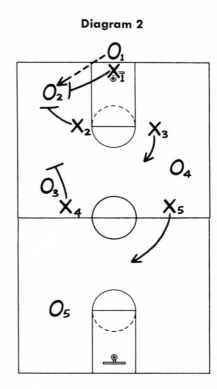

After the short pass in, X-1 follows the ball and with X-2 attempts to put the squeeze on the ball (Diagram 2). As this is happening, X-3 moves as shown. X-4 and X-5, at center court, tandem as shown in the diagram. If the pass is made back to O-1 (the easiest pass), then X-3 attacks and X-1 follows the ball and again we attempt the squeeze. X-2 now becomes a floater and X-4 comes up to stop O-2, while X-5 falls back to protect against any men deep such as O-5 (Diagram 3).

If O-2 escapes to the outside (we regard this as a sin for X-2—but it will happen) we use these shifts (Diagram 4): X-4 comes up and stops O-2's forward progress; X-2 squeezes; X-1 retreats down the middle watching the ball, X-3 holds and floats if there is still an offensive man back; and X-5 is guarding against the long pass.

If they beat our press, X-4's only responsibility is to prevent the layup until he gets help; he retreats inside the dotted line and under

Diagram 3	Diagram 4
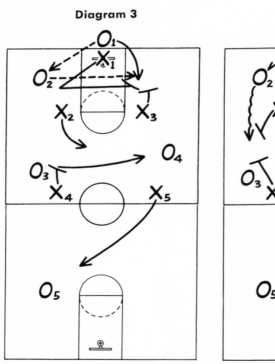	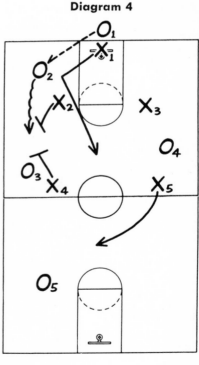

no circumstances does he attempt to stop even a six-foot jump shot. If a shot is taken he has two duties: (1) if the shot is missed, he rebounds and starts the fast break; (2) if the shot is made, he grabs the ball, steps out of bounds, and starts the fast break.

To me, two things are important for the success of any zone press:

1. The ability of the player to anticipate a pass before it is thrown, and I have come to conclude that mostly this is guesswork. The job is made easier if you are up against a team that uses a strict pattern on attack.
2. The ability of the player to *improvise*. It's impossible to tell players what to do in every situation, so I tell them to react and worry about whether it's right or wrong later.

Here are a few coaching conclusions on the zone press:

- *Don't Overcoach.* There are so many situations that the boy needs freedom to react without thinking.
- *Guard Against Carelessness.* The zone is dangerous if your boys are careless; they will get into foul trouble quickly.
- *Watch Tiredness:* In practice, don't let your players get overly tired.

As to practice, you'll find that it is a poor place to judge the effectiveness of your zone under playing conditions. (1) There's no screaming crowd to create pressure on the offense. (2) There's no public embarrassment in a defensive mistake or foul. (3) There's no opposing coach to get excited and, in turn, get his players excited.

7.

45.9 POINTS PER GAME

by ELDON MILLER

Head Basketball Coach
Wittenberg (Ohio) University

When Eldon Miller took over the reins at Wittenberg University for the 1962–63 season, he was in a tough spot; for the previous four years, Wittenberg, under Ray Mears, had led all the nation's small colleges on defense. But Coach Miller polished the Wittenberg record further: The 1962–63 Tigers were 26–2; rated the top small college team by most polls and extended the home court victory string to 66 games. Most important: they led all colleges on defense. His over-all coaching record is 61–12.

With each new season, defensive basketball is getting greater emphasis, and I feel the trend will continue. This is because players are improving offensively, and more and more coaches are using slow-down offensive tactics. Teams are being coached (Cincinnati is a prime example) to control the ball until they get the percentage shot. Defensing a control team is much more difficult and requires various defenses.

Before getting into our defensive system—which for five straight years has enabled us to lead the nation's small colleges in defense (and all colleges in 1962–63)—I want to mention two things which I feel are definite factors in our success:

1. Attitude: Some players, without encouragement, love defense because of its challenge; most, however, prefer offense because it

184

has appeal to the player and the public. A coach must sell defense. We emphasize defense in all practices, and stress defense to our players. One thing leads to another. We have built a record, a tradition, and a reputation for defense; our players all take pride in upholding them. Ed McClusky, famed defensive coach at Farrell, Pennsylvania, once said that he takes his five best defensive players and teaches them offense. There's a lot in it.

2. *Drills:* Effective defensive drills are a must, and we have two favorites:

(a) *One-on-one:* The offensive man takes the ball at the top of the key and dribbles. The defensive man must prevent him from getting a good shot and must get the ball. Even if the shot is made, both men scramble for the ball. As long as the offensive man gets the ball, he remains on offense.

We coach two important things: (1) The defensive man uses a parallel stance and concentrates on keeping good defensive position. He should be close enough to prevent the good shot before the drive, and far enough away to prevent any drive. His hands and arms move naturally at his sides unless the offensive man attempts a shot or commits a ball-handling error. (2) We do not reach in and try to steal the ball. Our experience is that such efforts result in footwork errors and easy baskets for the opposition.

(b) *Defensive footwork:* The offensive man takes the ball at one end of the court. He attempts to advance the ball over the midcourt line while the defensive man tries to delay him for 10 seconds. The offensive man has a tremendous advantage, and the defensive man must put forth all his strength. The drill is an excellent conditioner and should be used for all men; it will help you pick out your best defensive players.

In today's game, one defense will not be enough; it will not stymie all offenses. Our defense changes with each game and depends a lot on accurate scouting reports.

We start, however, with a basic 1-2-2 zone, and make our adjustments from it. The alignment is standard (Diagram 1). The deep men line up on the foul lanes approximately six to eight feet in front of the basket. The wing men line up two feet outside the lanes about fifteen feet from the basket. The point man takes his position at the top of the key.

From this alignment, we use both a straight zone and a combina-

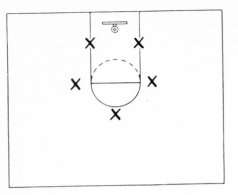

Diagram 1

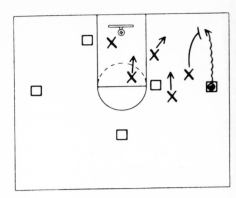

Diagram 2

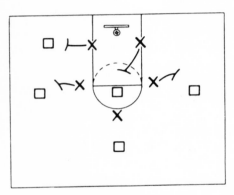

Diagram 3

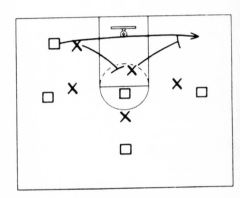

Diagram 4

Diagram 5

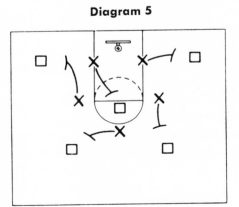

tion defense. The straight zone is relatively simple to teach, and has been very effective. Our zone rules are standard, with one exception:

When an offensive man dribbles to the corner from the outside, the wing man on that side will go with him and take him all the way. (Ordinarily, the deep man has the corner responsibility.) We make this exception because we have time to go with the driver in this situation, and want to keep our rebounders close to the basket (Diagram 2).

Other than this, our 1-2-2 follows all the basic rules.

Our combination defense is our most frequent defense, and the one in which the players have the most confidence. It is, however, difficult to teach, and I find it takes most players one full year to master it completely. It is important to master the 1-2-2 first, because it gives the players something to go back to if they become confused.

We start teaching our combination defense as soon as practice starts. First, we take the basic offensive alignments and learn how to shift to cover them.

Another name for our combination defense is the match-up zone; it is designed to give each of our players a man responsibility all of the time. They will not always be guarding the same man, but when a shot is taken, each will have an opponent to screen off the boards.

Here are three illustrations of shifts and switches:

1. When a game begins, we set up in our 1-2-2 until we make sure how our opponent is lining up. If, for example, they are using a 1-3-1 zone offense, we rotate so that we match up with them. (Diagram 3.) By this rotation, we eliminate the weakness we had at the high post and cover the opponents man-to-man.

2. If the opponent's low post man runs from corner to corner, our two deep men switch on him and the high post man. (Diagram 4.) The deep men must talk and work together exceptionally well to make a fast and effective switch.

3. We frequently see the 2-1-2 alignment on offense. In making our rotation to cover this, we always bring our smallest wing man out in order to keep the bigger player closer to the basket. (Diagram 5.)

The deep man that moves out must be capable of guarding an outside man.

Here are our four basic rules for our combination defense:

1. Turn all offensive men into the middle where you can get help.
2. When your man doesn't have the ball, slough toward the middle to help your teammates.
3. Don't let your man receive a pass if he is in good scoring position.
4. Spring back on defense and set up in the 1-2-2—*then* make the rotation.

Our combination defense is our best defense, and the players love it. It is a real challenge, because they must master new slides for each opponent.

I believe that the match-up zone will be used much more in coming seasons.

8.

DEFENSE AGAINST
THE FAST BREAK

by BOB VAUGHN

Head Basketball Coach
Surrattsville (Clinton, Maryland) High School

Bob Vaughn has been head basketball coach at Surrattsville High School since 1961. His record—77 wins against 32 losses, including three District II championships, three County championships and one State Class A championship.

Our system at Surrattsville High School for defense against the fast break is a very aggressive one. We believe in stopping the break before it can be organized. "Stop it before it starts," I tell our boys. And here's the way we do it—through four areas of defense:

1. Offensive Boards: Your opponent cannot break unless he has the ball. We feel that a strong offensive board charge will often stop their running game completely. Therefore, we send at all times three to four men on the offensive board, leaving many times only one back for defensive purposes. Most of the time our offensive rebounders outnumber the defensive rebounders four to three.

When you get the second and third shot over and over, the opponents will quickly forget their break. We rely on controlled offense to assure us of good offensive organization. At every point or option of our offense, we get good offensive board positions. Our board charge appears as shown in Diagram 1. Some coaches call this a 3½ offensive charge. I like to think of it as being four simply because the boy at the foul line is looking for the long rebound or the loose ball.

2. *Tying up the Rebounder:* When our opponent secures possession of the ball, we must clamp on him immediately since we only have one guard back. In Diagram 1, you saw how we set up our offensive board charge. We have a triangle set up with our fourth man backing up the triangle. When our opponent gets the rebound, the two closest men tie up the rebounder as shown in Diagram 2.

You see that on the rebound, players 1 and 3 immediately double team the defensive rebounder. Our main purpose here is to slow down the break and harass the rebounder so he cannot get the pass off. By doing this we force the opponent into a traveling violation. At times, the rebounder gets excited and throws a wild pass. This also gives us a chance for a tie up.

Problem: The big problem in the clamp seems to be the tendency to commit the foul because of over-aggressiveness. Your players must be indoctrinated with the idea that they *are not* trying to steal the ball—but simply trying to slow down the opponent's fast break and force them to make the mistake that will give your team the ball.

Note that while the double team is taking place, players 2 and 4 (Diagram 2) are hustling back on defense. I feel that if the clamp only holds them for a second or two, their break is stopped. We have done our job.

Rebound drill: Telling your players to clamp or double team is not enough. This maneuver under the boards must be drilled over and over so that your boys will simply react to it rather than go through the whole thought process. We use a common drill which is very simple (Diagram 3)—a 3 on 3 rebound drill.

The coach shoots the ball. A lid could be used over the basket. The defensive rebounder will attempt to get the ball then throw the outlet pass to the side to the coach, who is cutting to the side of the court where the ball is rebounded. The offense first tries for the tip, but if the opponent gets the ball he must clamp to stop the first outlet pass. We practice this drill normally five to ten minutes each practice session.

Benefits: This drill is also good for teaching defensive position, offense board charge, tipping, and for general overall aggressiveness.

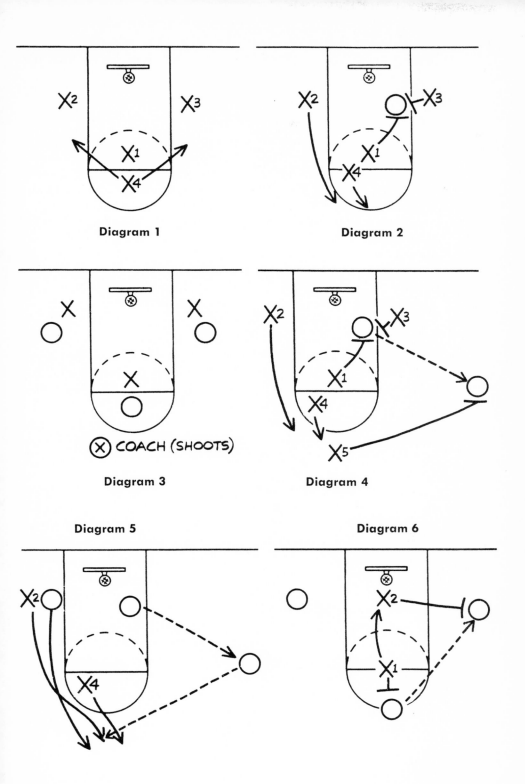

Diagram 1

Diagram 2

Diagram 3

ⓧ COACH (SHOOTS)

Diagram 4

Diagram 5

Diagram 6

3. Cutting off the Outlet Pass: Most teams that use the break as their primary offense organize their break. So before we play a team, we always have them scouted. We ask ourselves five questions:

1. Is their break organized?
2. Where is their outlet pass?
3. What about team speed?
4. Where do they like to shoot?
5. Do they dribble much?

Most all teams throw the outlet pass to the side. Most coaches agrees that a pass down the center is a dangerous one. The outlet pass is almost always on the same side that the rebound was obtained. This is where player 5 is used in defending a break. Player 5 wants to see which side the ball will rebound on. When the ball comes off the rim, he then goes in the same direction.

In Diagram 4, the ball is rebounded on 5's right; therefore, he knows that the outlet pass will probably be on the right side. He starts moving in that direction and can do one of two things: (1) If he gets the good angle, he can cut in front of the potential receiver and get the ball. This is demoralizing to a running team. (2) If he cannot get the ball, which happens in most cases, he must stop the outlet man from advancing up court. A good defensive maneuver is to come to a stop a few feet from the receiver. Many times he will turn into the defensive man giving them an offensive foul and you the ball.

After the ball is thrown to the outlet man on the side, teams have different methods of getting the ball down court. The great majority attempt to get the ball to the center and then get the three lanes filled. This gives players 2 or 4 a chance for an interception since they are falling back on defense. Some teams double up from the side. Of course, player 5's job is to prevent this. Other teams bring the ball up the side. Players 2 and 4 know this and hustle to cut off the pass (Diagram 5).

4. Tandem: This is our last line of defense against a fast break. Normally because of our method of defending the break, we get our big men back for this job. We place one man at the foul line and one man under the basket. Player 1 stops the dribble or ball handler. Player 2 takes the first pass. After the first pass, player 1 drops under the bucket. We are trying to get them to throw two or more passes to enable us to get defensive help up court (Diagram 6).

9.

THE MULTI-ZONE DEFENSE

by Warren Mitchell

Assistant Basketball Coach
Davidson (North Carolina) College

*In four years as head basketball coach at Newport News
(Virginia) High School, Warren Mitchell compiled an
overall record of 78 wins and 11 losses. During that time, his
teams advanced to the semi-finals of the state tourneys once
and were undefeated state champions in 1963–64. At present,
Warren Mitchell is assistant basketball coach at Davidson
College.*

Today, many coaches are turning to the multi-defenses in hopes of
stopping the good shooters and containing the highly organized
team. If you entertain thoughts of this nature, you'll want your
man-to-man and zone to start out with similar appearances—and
both to be sound.

In the 1963–64 regular basketball season, this zone with
match-up principles allowed our opponents 29.8 points per game, in
a district whose offensive average was 54 points per game.

On occasion we change from the multi-zone to a man-to-man. We
find that often after being in the zone for several minutes, it's easy
to go into man-to-man without our opponents recognizing it for a
time. Whenever your boys can do this successfully, they'll enjoy this
feeling of fooling the opponent. This had a positive effect on our
defensive morale and encouraged our boys to do even better.

Here are the rules for the multi-zone defense; diagram 1 illustrates the multi-zone set up:

RULES FOR D AREA

1. Man in D area with ball—he is covered by D.

2. Man in D area without ball—sag to ball but be in position to cover this man if he should get the ball.

3. If two men are in D's area, he will take man nearest "A" line.

4. Any time a single offensive man plays out front, D will take him as long as he remains in D area. (Note Diagram.) If he should dribble into E's area, E will take him and D will sag back and take next player in D area. This is an anticipated move by all members of the zone.

5. If D's man breaks through zone, D will go with him until he reaches A area, and then will release and return to sagging D area position.

6. Ball on opposite side of floor: (a) If ball is in C corner (position 4 or 6), D will take position in the middle of foul line. (b) If ball is in E area, D will sag to middle but must be in position to get to his man by the time the ball does.

7. Ball on same side of floor: (a) If ball is in B area (position 3), D will sag to middle and take next pass toward his area. (b) If ball is in B area (position 5), D will sag to middle of foul line and cover the second man to receive ball from the corner.

8. If ball is in E area and man in D's area should move toward and into B's area—D must sag back to position 1 to protect against lob pass and also be ready to pick up anyone that might come into his area.

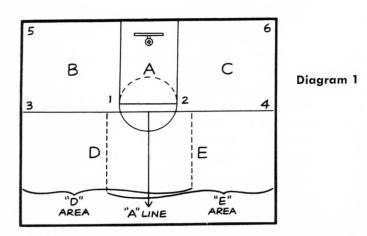

Diagram 1

RULES FOR E AREA

1. Man in E area with ball—he is covered by E.

2. Man in E area without ball—sag to ball but be in a position to cover this man if he should get the ball.

3. If there are two men in E area—E will take the man that will receive the first pass from D area.

4. If there is a one-man front—E will drop off to position 2 and pick up man who will receive first pass from D.

5. Any time a cutter leaves E area—E will go with him until he gets into A area, and then release and return to sagging E area position.

6. If cutter leaves E area and no one enters E area—E will take position 2, preventing lob pass and ready to take anyone who might break into E area.

RULES FOR B AREA

1. Man in B area with ball—he is covered by B.

2. Man in B area without ball—take position that will enable you to cover him quickly if he should receive the ball.

3. No opponent in B area and none in A area—B will take position in front of basket and help with any free lance judgment play.

4. If two men are in B area—B will take man at position 3.

5. Any time man in B area cuts for the basket, guard him until he is in A area and return to B area only if it becomes occupied.

RULES FOR C AREA

1. Man in C area with ball—he is covered by C.

2. Man in C area without ball—take position that will enable you to guard him quickly if he receives.

3. Two men in C area—C will take man who is in position to receive first pass from E area.

4. If man in C should break to opposite corner (B area), C will take position under basket and take any one coming into his area.

5. If man in C should break to opposite corner and no one comes into C area, he would take man in position 5 in B area.

6. If no one is in A area and man in C area should break to foul line, C will go with him. He now has A's responsibilities.

7. If C is guarding man in 4 position and pass should be made from him into position 6, C will "sandwich-in" between ball and basket and take A's responsibilities.

8. If ball is in D area and no one is in A area, C will pick up cutter from E or C area.

RULES FOR A AREA

1. Man in A area without ball—A will take him and prevent him from getting the ball.

2. No one is in area A and ball is in area E or D—sag your position toward deepest man in C or B area.

3. Two men in A area—take man nearest foul line area.

4. If ball is in E area and there is no one in A area, A is responsible for picking up any cutters coming from D or B areas.

5. If ball is in C area, A will zone area between ball and the basket and cover any passes going into position 6.

SITUATION RULE FOR A AND C

In rules for C (rule 7 concerning "sandwich")—when this occurs, the man directly guarding the man with the ball becomes the C man of the zone and follows his rules until another sandwich occurs. Ball in position 6—on the first pass out of corner toward E area, A man who is zoning area between position 6 and basket looks quickly to middle of A area. If there is a man there, he will take him; if not, his man will be in position 5 of B area.

10.

CHANGING DEFENSES

by BOB MULCAHY

Assistant Basketball Coach
University of Kansas

In five years as head basketball coach at Seneca (Louisville, Kentucky) High School, Bob Mulcahy compiled an over-all record of 125 wins and only 14 losses. Both his 1962–63 and 1963–64 squads won the state championship, and included 3 All-Americans and 4 All-Staters. At present, Bob Mulcahy is freshman basketball coach at the University of Kansas.

The basic basketball defense is, and probably always will be, the man-to-man. Our system of changing defenses is no great revolution, but simply a means of giving the defense some advantage over the offense by the element of surprise. In changing from man-to-man to zone, we always use the 2-3 alignment as illustrated in Diagrams 1, 2 and 3.

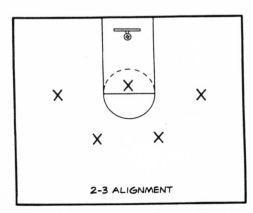

Diagram 1

197

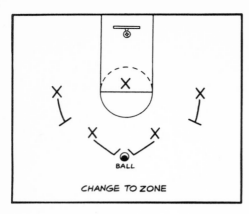

CHANGE TO ZONE

Diagram 2

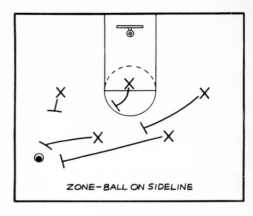

ZONE-BALL ON SIDELINE

Diagram 3

Diagram 4

Diagram 5

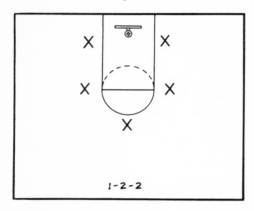

1-2-2

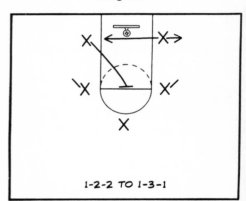

1-2-2 TO 1-3-1

- Diagram 1 illustrates our man-to-man defense in the 2-3 alignment.
- Diagram 2 illustrates our change to zone defense when the ball is in the front center of the court. The two guards trap the man with the ball and the forwards come high to prevent the outlet pass by covering possible next receivers.
- Diagram 3 illustrates our zone defense when the ball is on the side lines. Two guards trap the man with the ball, and the weak side forward comes high to prevent the cross-court pass.

Man-to-man to Zone: We use several different keys with which to change our defense from man-to-man to zone:

1. We call the defense from the bench.

2. Have a very capable player on the floor mix the defense at intervals. Such a boy usually plays against the best forward on the

198

opposing team. This puts him in a position to observe the offense coming up the floor and see where the ball is in relation to the center of the floor and also the side line.

3. We use the score board. When our score is an even number, we play man-to-man; when our score is an odd number, we play zone.

4. We also use the time on the score board—the minute digits.

5. We found through experience that the best method for us was to have a boy on the floor call the change by using a system of numbers, because we always wanted to zone trap when the ball was in front center, or could be trapped against the side lines.

Zone-to-Zone: For us, the 1-2-2 zone (Diagram 4) is the best because of its flexibility in adjustment and the option of being able to match the offensive alignment man-to-man, but still play zone principles. Our first method of playing zone defense out of the 1-2-2 is to place our two biggest men under the basket, and our third biggest at the point because he can cover more area with less movement than a smaller and even quicker boy. Our basic change out of the 1-2-2 set-up is to a 1-3-1 (Diagram 5). We do this by having the quicker of the two boys under the basket cover the base line, and the other boy cover the foul line area of the court any time the offense sends a man to the high post. We use the signal "middle" to let all our boys know there is an offensive man in the middle, and that we will be playing 1-3-1.

Our second method of changing zone to zone is to use the same principles as above, plus scouting information. We would have a team scouted to the point that we knew pretty well what they would do against a zone—as was the case in our final game of the state tournament last year. We knew that our opponent was too quick for us to play man-to-man, since we had two regulars at 6'8" and 6'9" who would be guarding boys 6'2" and 5'11" who were fast and excellent shooters. We also knew that they liked to surround the zone and have the 6'2" boy break to the high post from the right corner of the floor. So we decided to use our 1-2-2, not as we normally play it, but in a matching situation which would look like we were playing man-to-man. But when they went to the man on high post, our man would follow him and yell "middle" and we would retreat some and play our 1-3-1 zone. We won the game by 10 points and discovered another method of changing zone to zone.

11.

THE SWITCHING MAN-FOR-MAN DEFENSE

by MYNDRET C. BUSACK

Head Basketball Coach
Mitchell (Indiana) High School

Myndret C. Busack's 10-year record as head basketball coach at Adrian (Michigan) High School is 103 wins against 55 losses, and includes three regional championships, one state championship and one state runner-up. At present, Myndret Busack is head basketball coach at Mitchell High School.

Ours is an offensive defense. We are always alert for opportunities to place the offense at a disadvantage, and always looking for that advantageous defensive point at which to apply pressure. We are fast break conscious and believe that we can accomplish our objectives by switching whenever two men cross at the ball. Our players away from the ball must sag toward it.

Our defensive philosophy is based on the following—(a) master the individual fundamentals; (b) drill and practice game-like situations; (c) follow the rules of sound basketball defense. Here's the way we go about perfecting this philosophy.

Fundamentals: Our work on defensive fundamentals may be different than most high school coaches use—for instance,

1. *Running*—We work to toughen the feet by doing a lot of running before we begin to use any kind of a shuffle drill. Our first step is to set up a full-court one-on-one in which the defensive player

must keep his hands behind his back; the offensive player is limited to a particular area for this purpose. We progress to a two-on-two and a three-on-three, still keeping our hands behind our backs—but we have our players switch any time two men cross. We limit the amount of the dribble and allow only short passes. We progress to allowing the defensive players to use their hands as in normal defense.

2. *Stance*—We encourage the defensive stance in which the inside foot is forward and the inside hand is up. When it's not possible to get in this position, our players manage the job by doing what comes naturally. We want the knees flexed, tail down and the hands up and free for quick movement. The weight should be more on the back than forward. The fingers should be comfortably spread. We instruct our boys that they should try to flick the ball away with an upward swipe, and to yell "ball" when they have done so.

Drills: When we feel that the condition of the feet permits it, we begin to use the defensive shuffle drill—reacting to a dribbler or to directions from the coach. We work at this until we're able to go for about 90 seconds. Next, we stress the following drills:

1. *Situation*—We do a great amount of two-on-two in the offensive court in order to get our players acquainted with the various situations they will meet. Drill situations are set up in which we do the following: (a) guard to guard; (b) guard to forward; (c) guard to pivot; (d) forward to pivot.

2. *High post split*—We then progress to defensing the high post split (Diagram 1). To combat this, we try to keep the ball from the high post man by playing tough at the passing lane. In defensing the split, we have our defensive men drop back to their side of the high post—and take the first cutter to his side and force him wide and out of the lane. The post defender has to take the second cutter to the same side, and the third man must cut off the post man's roll to the basket.

3. *Switch*—We try to anticipate the necessity of the switch. To drill for our switching defense, we set up a five-on-five situation without the ball, and designate the offensive and defensive groups. The offense is constantly moving or running in a helter-skelter pattern. We switch whenever two men cross. The most difficult offensive maneuver for us to meet in our switching defense is the

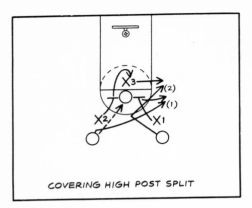

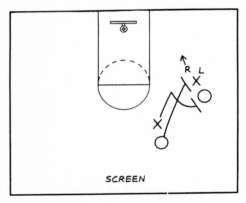

Diagram 1

COVERING HIGH POST SPLIT

Diagram 2

JUMP SWITCH

Diagram 3

SCREEN

Diagram 4

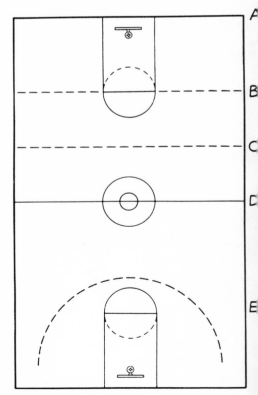

screen and roll. We try to defend against this by means of an aggressive jump switch (Diagram 2). Our defender on the man setting the screen will alert his teammate through talking, and will jump quickly out into the path of the dribbler and dominate him to remove his thoughts from that of passing to the roller. We hope to get a jump ball, a traveling or dribbling violation, or a charging foul from this action.

4. *Screen*—Our defense on the roller is based upon two ideas: (1) The defensive man upon whom the screen has been set is to drop his foot nearer to the screener and face him, being alert to beat him to the best path to the basket; (2) Our pivot defender is alert to pick up the roller in the event that he gets away; he is to step into his path, or "check the cutter," as we call this action (Diagram 3). The defensive man who has been screened and can't beat the roller to the best path is to "peel to the baseline," going inside and pivoting inside with his inside hand down.

Rules: With these basic ideas in mind, we stress the following rules for sound basketball defense:

A. General Rules

1. Make everything go inside.
2. No one ever turns the corner on the baseline drive.
3. Drop off and toward the ball—prevent lay-up shots.
4. Drop back to the line of the ball.
5. Short pivot area—play in front of your man toward the ball.
6. Make everyone cut behind you.
7. Beat your man to the ball on cuts from the weak side.
8. Pressure the man with the ball.
9. Drive your man according to the scouting report.
10. Force the cross-dribble.
11. Give the opponent only one way to go.
12. Dominate your opponent.

B. Baseline Rules

1. Beat your man to the spot.
2. Always give him only one way to go—inside.
3. Drive toward help.
4. Put pressure.

Pressure Type Defense: Here's how we put pressure on the man with the ball. We divide the basketball court into five areas, at which points we apply our pressure type defense (Diagram 4).

A—Our pressure is on the man who has the ball out of bounds, and all men in bounds.

B—Our pressure line is the defensive line extended.

C—Our pressure line is an imaginary line midway between the free-throw line extended and the mid-court line.

D—Our pressure line is the mid-court line.

E—Our pressure will be applied at about twenty-three feet out from the basket—we wish to prevent any pass or drive to the key-hole area.

Other Tips: We switch on any crossing at the ball trying to use an aggressive jump switch. We use the sideline areas and the various corner pockets as areas to drive the man with the ball, so as to set up an opportunity for a double-team. Our defenders are instructed to call for "help" whenever they have the offense at a great disadvantage. We also double-up whenever the chance permits. "Talk" to communicate information adds to making our defense strong.

12.

DEFENSE: DESIRE, DISCIPLINE, DRILLS

by DICK CAMPBELL

Head Basketball Coach
Carson-Newman (Jefferson City, Tenn.) College

Three years ago, successful coach Dick Campbell decided to place major emphasis on defense. Since then, his Carson-Newman College Eagles have won three conference titles, two conference tournaments, three NAIA District 27 titles, and three trips to the NAIA national tournament. At Carson-Newman, Coach Campbell's record is 154–45. He was named 1965 "Coach of the Year" by the NAIA.

At Carson-Newman we basically play man-to-man defense, but with variations: sometimes pressure, sometimes sloughing. We sprinkle in zones if it fits our opposition. Sometimes we mix zones, man-to-man and presses. We call our defense a Kamikaze Defense, because we put the job ahead of ourselves.

I won't try to tell you how to play defense. I am convinced that defense is the key to success; we changed from a good club to a championship club when we began to place prime emphasis on defense. I think these elements are the basis of a successful defensive team.

1. Desire: The boys have to *want* to play defense, and this runs counter to the natural instinct, which is offense and shooting. The coach, therefore, must be convinced of defense himself, and sell it to the boys. Here are some things to build up this desire. After a game or two, when the players can see the results, some of the problems are over. Players, students, fans and the papers will pick up what you are trying to do and will help carry the ball.

    a. At our first squad meeting, we talk mostly about defense, and set our goal for the season. I let the players set this target; if it is their choice, they will work harder to achieve it and have the necessary desire.

    b. We tell the boys that defense is 90% desire and 10% fundamentals; the ratio may be high, but it helps impress the importance of desire.

    c. Our most coveted award at the end of the season is the best defensive player trophy. I believe that now every boy on our squad would rather win this than any other award.

    d. The boys know that if they can't or won't play defense, they will spend most of the season on the bench.

    2. *Discipline:* I am convinced that unless you discipline your offense, you cannot have a great defensive team. We tell our boys that they must get the good percentage shot every time they get the ball; it is an unpardonable sin to make a bad pass, travel, double dribble, palm the ball, or take a poor percentage shot.

    3. *Drills:* I am sure that many players do not play sound defense because of lack of desire, but because they are not in condition to maneuver like a good defense man should. Check up on your own drills; how many of them require the player to run backward instead of forward, laterally or at an angle with his back to the basket.

    So, at the beginning of practice, we put the ball on the rack and go to work on individual defense. Here are a few of our drills:

    a. *Back up:* Each player takes his defensive stance and backs up as fast as he can while maintaining good balance and proper defensive position (Diagram 1).

    b. *Oblique:* Players take defensive stance and move obliquely, using a slide step, being careful not to cross the feet. The second man begins when the first man gets to the top of the circle (Diagram 2).

    c. *Lateral:* Players take defensive stance facing coach, and move laterally across the floor, using the slide step. The coach can change direction by using the whistle (Diagram 3).

    d. *Combination:* Players take defensive stance and on hand signal

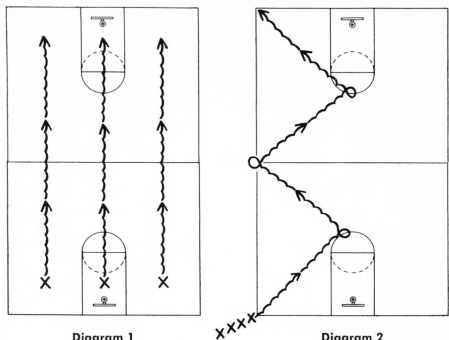

Diagram 1

Diagram 2

Diagram 3

Diagram 4

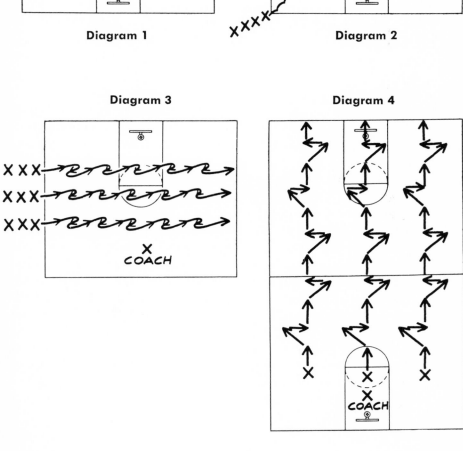

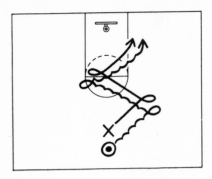

Diagram 5

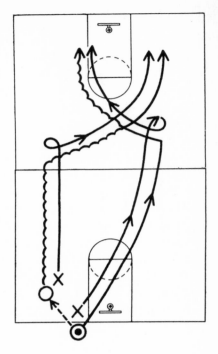

Diagram 6

Diagram 7

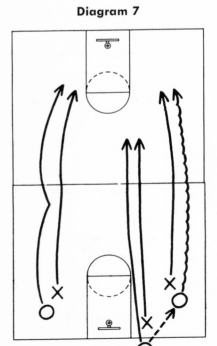

Diagram 8

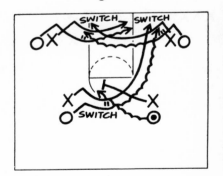

from coach move backwards, obliquely, and laterally until they have covered the court (Diagram 4).

Later we begin work on our 1-on-1, 2-on-2, 3-on-3, and 4-on-4 defensive drills.

e. *1-on-1:* I believe the 1-on-1, half or full court, is the best way to teach a boy sound individual defense. It is one of the finest drills I know. Each boy is on his own. Offensive man O with ball tries to score on defensive man D. D tries to stop O's dribble and prevent the shot (Diagram 5).

f. *2-on-2:* In the 2-on-2 we begin to work on the switch and slide-through and usually run this drill full court with automatic switching in the backcourt (Diagram 6).

g. *3-on-3:* Our 3-on-3 is usually full court and we tell our boys to switch automatically in the backcourt and we also begin to teach the boys to look for the double team situation (Diagram 7).

h. *4-on-4:* Our 4-on-4 is usually half court and here we teach switching, sliding-through, double-teaming and looking for blind picks and how to defense the four-man weave (Diagram 8).

The real purpose of our defense is to force the opponent to do things he doesn't want to do. For example, if a defensive guard likes to go right, we try to force him to go left. If a team starts its patterns with a guard-to-forward pass, we overplay the forwards and the passing guard. If the opponent doesn't play well when picked up tight, our guards go to get them at mid-court and everyone puts pressure on his man.

INDEX